My Son Eric

My Son Eric

by Mary V. Borhek

The Pilgrim Press ● Cleveland, Ohio

The Pilgrim Press, Cleveland, Ohio 44115
© 1979 by Mary V. Borhek
All rights reserved. Published 1979
Printed in the United States of America
The paper used in this publication is acid free and meets the minimum
requirements of American National Standard for Information Sciences-
Permanence of Paper for Printed Library Materials, ANSI Z39.48-1984

98 97 96   10 9 8 7 6 5

Library of Congress Cataloging-in-Publication Data
Borhek, Mary V   1922-
        My son Eric.
        Includes bibliographical references.
        1. Homosexuals—United States. 2. Homosexuals—United
States—Family relationships. I. Title.
HQ76.3.U5B67 301.41'57'0924 79-16161
ISBN 0-8298-0372-6
ISBN 0-8298-0729-2 (pbk.)

To Lee
who walked with me in the dark places
and held the lamp
that I might see to fight my way
upward

Contents

1

The X
Factor

It had been a pleasant Saturday. In the morning Emily, my daughter, had gone off to her job at the Art Institute. Hans, my son-in-law, a graduate student at The University of Illinois, was working on a paper in his study, so I had the living room with its fold-out sofa bed to myself.

This was my first visit to Emily's and Hans's apartment in Chicago. They had been married in June. Now it was February, and I had driven down from Minneapolis to see them. I had brought along several books, and I spent the morning enjoying the luxury of reading in bed with no household chores to nag me.

In the afternoon Hans took me to the Museum of Science and Industry, where we saw several of the exhibits, including the coal mine. In the evening we talked and listened to records. About midnight we all went to bed.

There had been one rather unusual occurrence at the museum. When Hans and I were down in the mock coal mine we had to get into little tramcars. There was a long seat running lengthwise on each side of the car, and because our tour was so crowded the guide told us to slide down as far as we could to make room for more people.

As I was sliding down the bench toward the end of the car I suddenly had a funny light-headed feeling, and I thought with a shock of déjà vu, "I dreamed this." How long ago I had dreamed it I had no idea. The dream had been lost to my conscious mind, as most dreams are. But now in the dim light, as I looked out the open sides of the tram at the mock coal face, I knew I had experienced the whole scene before.

I hadn't the slightest idea why I should have dreamed of the coal mine at the Museum of Science and Industry in Chicago when I had never seen it before that afternoon. I mentioned the peculiar incident to Hans later in the afternoon as we were driving back to the apartment. He couldn't offer much help as to why I should have had this odd experience.

*   *   *   *

I was wakened by the ringing of a phone. It was ringing persistently in Hans's study. Emily padded out of the bedroom and into the study. I heard her say, "I'll call him."

She roused Hans. They went into the study and closed the door.

I lay there on the sofa bed in the living room listening. The clock showed one-thirty. Who in the world was calling at one-thirty in the morning? Hans wasn't saying much. Apparently the person at the other end was doing most of the talking. Now and again I would hear him say something briefly in a low tone.

I waited. The clock ticked on. Everything inside me was cold and still. This was no casual chat from a Chicago friend. Was it Hans's grandmother on the West Coast? Not likely. If she called at that hour, it would be an emergency and they would not talk on and on. The same thing was true if it were his parents in Virginia. That left—

That left Eric and Barbara. Eric was my nineteen-year-old son, who had his own apartment south of Minneapolis. Barbara was my sixteen-year-old daughter.

Three and one-half years earlier my husband, Tom, had

resigned as pastor of his congregation in the suburb of Lakota, north of Minneapolis, and had divorced me. He had moved to St. Paul, but Barbara and I had remained in Lakota. She was home alone this weekend, having resisted my suggestion that she might like to have a friend stay with her. "I'm not a baby anymore," she had protested.

Had something happened to Barbara? Why did the phone conversation go on and on?

I couldn't lie still any longer. I got out of bed and walked a few steps back and forth beside the bed, stiff with fear and shivering with both cold and fright. It was Eric or Barbara, one or the other. Had there been an automobile accident?

Something kept me from going to the door of the study, knocking, and asking what was going on.

At last I climbed back, shivering, under the covers. I looked at the clock. It was quarter after two. Forty-five minutes since the phone had rung. I heard Hans's low voice say something, and then there was the almost imperceptible sound of the phone being set in its cradle.

I waited. Now they would come out of the study, and I could call Emily and ask her what was wrong. But they didn't. They remained in the study. Now and again I could hear their murmured voices.

"I shall shortly go out of my mind," I thought. I felt suffocated. I *had* to know.

"Emily," I called softly.

There was no answer. Everything was silent. Perhaps she had not heard me. I had the feeling that she had but that she was delaying the evil moment as long as possible.

"Emily," I called again a little louder.

She came swiftly, as if she knew the game was up.

"What is it?" I asked.

Wordlessly she turned and went back to the study and came out with Hans. They stood together beside the sofa bed.

"Who *was* it?" I asked.

Hans answered, "It was Barbara."

"What happened? Is she all right?" The weight on my chest was making it difficult to breathe.

I remembered the spaghetti party she had planned to have that evening. We had discussed it before I left, and I had given her permission to have it. She had asked if they might have wine with the dinner, and I had said no.

"We're not going to get drunk or anything," she had said with scorn.

"*You* may not get drunk," I had said, "but sometimes you can't control what another person is going to do. Besides, you're all under age."

There had been no more argument about wine.

But had she in the end served wine? Or had one of the guests supplied it? Had there been an accident?

"What *happened?*" I repeated. "Here, sit down," and I moved to make room for them to sit on the bed.

Hans sat down at the head end and drew his legs up under him. Emily perched at the foot like a small, tentative bird, ready to fly at a moment's notice.

"Is anybody hurt?" I asked. I felt as if I were trying to push an enormous boulder uphill and could hardly budge it.

"No, no one was hurt," Hans said.

"Then what happened?"

"Barbara was getting ready for the spaghetti supper, and Eric dropped in with a friend and spoiled it for her."

"Eric dropped in?" I said in amazement. It was a good forty minutes from Eric's apartment, and he was not in the habit of coming without a reason.

"He wanted to do his wash and brought the friend along to see the house."

"He wanted to do his wash!" I exclaimed, perplexed. He never came to the house just to do his laundry. It did not pay, either in time or in money, to drive up only for the sake of using my machine. "But why did that spoil the party?"

"Barbara didn't like the friend."

"Eric and the friend came to the party?"

"No, they came before the party. While she was getting ready."

It didn't make sense. Not just the facts that Hans was giving me. There was some X factor, some unknown that would put the whole thing in perspective. Hans and Emily knew what the X was, but they were not telling me.

Why had Eric come visiting when I was gone? It wasn't because he was devoted to Barbara. When they had any contact at all, they were at each other's throat. He had brought the friend "to see the house." But my house was small and unspectacular. Why did he want his friend to see the house?

The friend. Who was the friend? I knew Eric had new friends, but he had told me almost nothing about them. Was this friend male or female?

"Hans," I said, "is the friend a man or a woman?"

"A man," Hans replied.

How strange, I thought, for Eric to bring a man friend to see the house. If it was a girl he was interested in, I could understand that he might want her to see his home. But another man?

Another man.

What if— No, it couldn't be. *It couldn't be.* And yet for a long time there had been a nagging, unnamed fear buried deep within me, an unacknowledged awareness that in some way Eric was . . . different.

"Hans," I heard myself saying, "is Eric a homosexual?"

There was silence except for the chattering of Hans's teeth. The bed shook slightly because both he and Emily were shivering. The silence continued.

I knew the answer, but I had to hear it in words.

"Hans," I said again, "is Eric a homosexual?"

Again the silence and the uncontrollable shivering. Now I was sure.

"Then he is," I said.

"I promised him I wouldn't tell you," Hans said miserably.

"You didn't tell me," I said. "Your silence did." But even as I said it I knew that Hans could have denied it, and I would still have known. Something deep inside, an accumulation of things too small for anyone but a mother to notice, had made me ask that fateful question. Hans's answer had not really surprised me. It had confirmed something that had lain hidden in the shadows of my mind, an old unspoken intuition.

Deep in some subterranean level, I had known.

2

The Long Night

For a few minutes none of us spoke. There were no words that could possibly encompass that moment. I held out my arms, and Hans, Emily, and I held each other tightly while my tears flowed. At last we relaxed our embrace, and I reached for a tissue to wipe my tears.

"Thank God you two were with me when I found out," I said. "I don't have to go through the dark tunnel all by myself."

The dark tunnel. The coal mine. At some earlier time in a dream I had been in the coal mine at the museum. Down somewhere in my unconscious I had stepped out of time sequence and had seen ahead. "Yea, though I walk through the valley of the shadow of death, I will fear no evil: for thou art with me."[1] God had known all along. God had prepared everything for this moment of my knowing.

Suddenly I remembered the difficulties we had had in planning my trip to Chicago. One thing after another had postponed it. Finally I had been scheduled to visit the weekend before this. Emily had managed to get that Saturday and Sunday off from work. At the last minute the weather service had predicted blizzards, and so my visit had been moved to the present weekend. Had we, without knowing it, been operating on God's timetable?

Another verse flashed into my mind, illuminated with a depth of meaning I had not known before: "Surely he has borne our griefs and carried our sorrows."[2] God was *present*. God *knew*. The Almighty was bearing my grief and my sorrow. In the deepest sense I was not alone.

Even though it was two-thirty in the morning and Emily had to work the next day, we settled down to talk. There was no thought of sleep just then, no possibility of relaxing. Hans and Emily wrapped themselves in blankets and sat on the bed. I lay down again under the covers. I felt suddenly cold and weak.

"Tell me what happened with Barbara this evening," I said.

Hans explained that at about five o'clock, as Barbara was getting things ready for the spaghetti party, Eric had turned up with Brian "to show him the house" and to do his laundry. Barbara had been less than cordial. She told them to get out, that she was going to have a party and she didn't want them there.

Brian had replied that he didn't see any problem; Eric would fit in with the boys, and he would fit in with the girls. This had driven Barbara wild. They had ignored her pleas to leave. Eric had shown Brian the house (but not Barbara's room—she had marched upstairs, closed the door, and stood in front of it until they went downstairs again) and had then put a load of laundry in to wash.

"The noises in the basement upset Barbara a good deal," Hans said.

"What was going on down there?" I asked. I wanted to know exactly what she had been subjected to.

There did not seem to be any very clear information as to what exactly had been going on. But the sounds had upset her. Eventually the two men left for a while.

The guests arrived. In the middle of dinner Eric and Brian

returned, collected the laundry, and left, apparently without any untoward remarks or behavior. But Barbara was in terror the whole time that her guests would discern the real state of affairs, and though nothing happened outwardly, the evening for her was ruined. After the guests left, she called Hans and poured out her troubles to him.

"Did Barbara know before this about Eric?" I asked.

"Yes," Hans replied. "He told her last August. That's why she didn't want to go to Stone Harbor with him last Labor Day. She figured he would simply argue his point with her all the way there and back."

I remembered the episode clearly. She and Eric had talked of driving over to Lake Michigan to visit their grandmother, Tom's mother, who lived at Stone Harbor. Hans and Emily were going to be there also, and I had not understood why Barbara had not wanted to go too. She had not seen her grandmother for more than a year, and it would also be a chance to see Emily and Hans.

She had not gone. In answer to my attempts at persuasion she had simply said, "I don't want to go. I'm not going."

"Why not?" I had asked.

But Barbara and I had long ago ceased to be on terms where she confided in me. We existed side by side in the same house, but I was under no illusions as to how she felt about me. Basically I represented the authority against which she rebelled.

It was small comfort to know that Tom was no better off than I. She was distant from both of us, rebelling against everything I said and ignoring Tom unless he called her. I could never quite forget her wild, desolate wailing the night two years after Tom's and my divorce when he had told her and Eric that he was going to marry Meta. Somehow in that weeping was crystallized all the pain of the divorce, all the agony of the two years following the divorce while I clutched the shred of hope that Tom would return to his family.

With her friends Barbara displayed a sort of hard gaiety.

9

With me she was mostly sullen and uncommunicative. With Tom she was polite and dutifully agreeable. How much was her behavior caused by normal adolescent growing pains, and how much by the damage of divorce? I had no way of knowing.

"When did *you* find out about Eric?" I asked now, returning to the present.

Hans answered, "You remember the night the week before our wedding when Eric walked me home?" I did.

Emily had decided to be married at Trinity College chapel in Mount Hope, Virginia, rather than at our home in Lakota. It made sense. Mount Hope was my hometown; during her four years of college it had become Emily's home. Hans's home was in a neighboring town, where his father was pastor at the time. Almost all their friends were nearby.

During the week before the wedding we were staying in various parts of Mount Hope. Emily and Barbara stayed with Tom's cousins Peter and Julie Nilsson; Eric and I, with longtime friends of mine; and Hans, with one of the professors at the college.

Hans continued, "That night Eric told me that he had some suspicions that he had homosexual tendencies and asked if he could talk to my dad. I said of course, and we decided that I would alert Dad to make an opportunity to talk with Eric alone. I did—do you remember when they went to get gas in the car together?"

I nodded, feeling a fleeting moment of pity for Hans. To learn three days before his wedding that his new brother-in-law was probably homosexual must have been a shock.

"Dad suggested he talk with Henry Hilke, because he had had more counseling experience along this line than Dad had had." Henry had been a pastor, had gone into counseling work, and was now dean at the college.

I remembered Eric's setting up an appointment with Henry for the Sunday morning after the wedding, because we were leaving Mount Hope that afternoon. The friends with whom we were staying were at church, and I was upstairs packing. Eric and Henry went to the basement recreation room. I knew only that Eric was having trouble "finding himself."

I could identify with that only too well, and I knew that questioning him about it would be no help to him. It was the first time I could remember that Eric had not blurted out to me what was on his mind. I could only stand aside and be glad that he was doing something constructive about whatever was bothering him.

"Did you know about it then too?" I asked Emily.

She shook her head. "I found out in August, and I talked with him about it at Stone Harbor in September."

During the summer, I remembered, I had begun to have difficulty finding Eric home when I phoned. He had a full-time job during the summer, but he never seemed to be home in the evenings. When I did manage to reach him he often seemed in a hurry, and we did not have long conversations.

Once when he came to Lakota for a meal he mentioned that he had found some new friends. At one time he would have told me about them without my asking. Now he told me nothing, and I found that I did not know how to phrase questions so that they did not sound prying. Suddenly there was a shadow between us which I could not define.

Once I did ask if the friends were male or female, and he said a few of each. In time he mentioned some names: Jim, Gary, Scott. I ventured the remark that I bet most of these new friends were older than he was, and he said they were. It figured. Eric had never fitted with his peers. I had hoped that in college he would find some kindred spirits, but though he attended college classes, he was scarcely involved otherwise on campus because he also worked part-time at Honeywell.

I remembered that Eric had wanted to go see Hans and Emily in Chicago over Thanksgiving, taking his prospective new apartment mate, Roger, with him. Somehow things did not work out with Roger—he never did move in with Eric—and in

11

the end Barbara and Eric had gone to Chicago to spend Thanksgiving at Hans's and Emily's. What a nice time the four young people would have together, I thought.

When Eric dropped Barbara off that Sunday night, I was surprised and disappointed to discover that all four of them had apparently had a miserable time. They seemed to have spent the weekend largely in verbal combat, with the consensus being that I was fonder of Eric than of the girls and that I had spoiled him. I absorbed this blow as I had absorbed so many other blows—by saying nothing, explaining my reasons only to myself, then tucking the incident away in a corner of my mind.

Early in December, Eric talked with me about not continuing in college for the present. "I really have trouble concentrating and writing papers," he said. "I go to classes, then dash off to work. Then if I get together with my friends in the evening, I have to come home and try to hit the books, and it's just too much."

"I suppose most of your friends work and aren't in school any longer," I said.

"Yes, they don't have to go home and study. Besides, if I were getting what I wanted at school it might be different, but I'm not."

I could understand all these things only too well, or so I thought. For most of his life, Eric had had few or no close friends. From ninth grade on, he had had casual friends at school but no one with whom he got together after school hours to work on cars, to watch TV, or to go to the movies. Now at last he had friends. I could see that they might be pretty important to him.

I also knew that Eric and the head of the art department at college (art was Eric's major) had widely divergent views. Dr. Fremont was heavy on classical art: Greek, Roman, Renaissance. Eric wanted to concentrate on contemporary art in a variety of mediums. These were beneath Dr. Fremont's notice.

Because of his extremely high marks and ability, Eric had been awarded a very comprehensive scholarship.

"The one thing you must consider, Eric," I said, "is that if you interrupt your college education now, you will lose your scholarship, and you won't get it back."

I used the word interrupt instead of "drop out" because I did not believe he was the ordinary dropout. I thought it was more as if Eric were taking a leave of absence.

"I know," he said. "I've thought of that. It's so bad, though, that I don't even know if I can finish the term."

"You have only three more weeks of this term," I said. "You've already put in almost four months of it. Why don't you try to finish this term, and then you'll have a year and a half of college credits."

As it turned out, he did manage to stick it out for another three weeks, but that was as much as he could tolerate. By Christmas he knew that he would take a "leave of absence" from college and that he would have to find a full-time job with some other company because Honeywell had no full-time opening for him.

Christmas that year was a pretty dismal affair. Eric, Barbara, and I could not go to Chicago because of work schedules, and Emily and Hans could not come to Lakota for the same reason. So the three of us spent a somewhat gloomy Christmas Eve and Christmas Day together.

This was the first time there had been only the three of us on Christmas Eve. We went to the early Christmas Eve service, more because it was the thing to do on Christmas Eve than because we really wanted to go. Afterward we opened our gifts rather perfunctorily. I kept up a determinedly cheerful front in the face of a bleakness which was not helped by Eric's and Barbara's covert sniping at each other.

About half-past ten Barbara departed with friends for a late Christmas Eve service, and Eric and I were left alone.

Somehow the conversation that had once flowed so easily between Eric and me was now rather halting. There was an invisible barrier. We talked desultorily and soon went to bed. I didn't hear Barbara come in.

We made it through Christmas Day. Barbara was sullen, Eric depressed. There seemed to be more than the usual sibling rivalry flowing between them. "If I can only get through this day," I said to myself grimly, "I can go to work tomorrow and forget all this. Thank God, Christmas will be over and I don't have to cope with it for another year."

Even the meal was dispirited. I had bought a frozen turkey roast instead of bothering with a whole bird. The roast was ersatz, tasteless, and rubbery. Somehow it was the epitome of the whole day.

"So you two and Barbara knew about Eric," I said, coming back to the present of Hans, Emily, and myself at 3:30 A.M. in the darkened living room of their Chicago apartment. "Does Tom know?"

"Yes, Eric told him awhile back."

"What did Tom say?" I asked.

Hans shrugged. "Not too much."

I was surprised. I would have expected more of a reaction. He had always seemed to be harder on Eric than on the girls. But I knew that Tom saw Eric periodically, so to an extent Tom had apparently accepted the state of affairs.

"Everyone else knew but me," I said.

"It was only because Eric was afraid of your religious scruples. He was afraid you would either disown him or flip."

I nodded slowly. I understood what Hans was talking about, what Eric feared, and I could not blame him. I had on occasion expressed myself about homosexuality in the terms used in the Bible: it was "an abomination,"[3] and homosexuals need not think they would inherit the kingdom of God.[4]

I knew that homosexuality was one of the most difficult things to "cure"—much more difficult than drug addiction, according to David Wilkerson, who had dealt in depth with both conditions at his Teen Challenge center in New York City.[5] But I had a firm belief that Jesus could deal with homosexuality and could heal it as he could everything else. The person had only to ask for healing. It was as simple as that.

Eric's fear that I might "flip" was not an idle one. At one point in my life I had spent five years, off and on, under psychiatric care. When Tom had divorced me, I had almost died of various physical ailments, though mentally I had steeled myself against any renewed symptoms of nervous breakdown. Even now I was on medication for high blood pressure. I was able to work only three days a week because I simply did not have the physical stamina to manage more.

Again tears ran down my cheeks, and I realized suddenly how exhausted I was. But at least Eric had withheld the truth from me because he cared what I thought, not because he didn't.

I held out my arms again. I needed to be touched and held. Hans and Emily embraced me, and then they padded off to bed. It was now four o'clock in the morning. Emily had to get up at seven. Up until this point it had been a very long night. Now it would become a very short one.

3

"My Son, My Son!"

We were up again at seven. I hoped Hans and Emily had slept more than I had. Probably I dozed for an hour or so. Most of the time I was fitting together scattered pieces of a jigsaw puzzle. These pieces had been floating around in my head for years. Now, one by one, they were dovetailing into the completed framework that had just been given me.

Emily had said I need not get up just because she had to go to work. But they were tiptoeing back and forth through the living room between kitchen and bedroom. Besides that, my stomach was telling me it needed food. My eyes burned with fatigue and with shed and unshed tears, but sleep was impossible.

We had oatmeal with raisins. Surprisingly, it tasted good to me; I could not have managed anything more complicated. Hans drove Emily to work.

"Would you like to go back to sleep now?" he asked when he returned. "And what about going to church?"

"I couldn't possibly do either at this point," I told him. "But if you can, don't worry about me."

In the end we washed up the few breakfast dishes, and then we sat and talked.

16

"There was always something about Eric that seemed to demand so much of me," I told Hans. I realized with a little shock that his demands had begun soon after conception. "I had more trouble when I was pregnant with him than I did when I was pregnant with either of the girls. It wasn't a whole lot easier after he was born, either," I went on. "He had a lot of physical problems."

How could any child who was basically healthy have had so many problems, I wondered. When he was only a couple weeks old he developed a mouth fungus. This was only a minor, temporary difficulty.

Of far longer duration were Eric's feeding problems. I began by breast-feeding him. During the first month of his life he was on what seemed like a two-hour feeding schedule, night and day. Cereal did not help fill him up; it only gave him diarrhea. When he was a month old, in desperation one evening I mixed up a bottle of formula and fed it to him. He drank it down eagerly. After that he wanted only the bottle.

"Ordinary formula didn't agree with him," I told Hans, "so we tried all the canned and powdered substitutes. We finally settled on the one that disagreed with him least. Eventually the pediatrician suggested bringing milk just to a boil. I did that until Eric was more than a year old."

"Where was Emily while all this was going on?" Hans asked.

"Oh, she was there, but I'm afraid she got rather short shrift. Eric was more helpless and screamed louder." I felt a twinge as I remembered their opinions at Thanksgiving that I was fonder of Eric than of the others and had spoiled him. Was I really fonder, or had he demanded more, even at the age of a few weeks?

"Feeding wasn't the only problem," I continued. "When he began to teethe, he became hyper. He couldn't fall asleep. We eased every tooth into his head with aspirin and a sedative that the doctor prescribed.

"Another time he developed an iron deficiency, which made him even more hyper. He had to be hospitalized and given intravenous iron feedings."

I fell silent for a minute, remembering the many difficulties of Eric's first year of life.

"The feeding problem kept right on," I resumed.

"Yes," said Hans feelingly, "I know." He was well acquainted with Eric's limited food repertoire.

"I realize now what I did wrong," I said, "but at the time, because of my own psychological problems, I wasn't able to do anything different."

Between nine months and a year, Eric had suddenly stopped eating almost everything. I was unable to do what Dr. Spock recommended: simply remove the spurned food with no comment, and give the child nothing to eat until the next meal. Earnestly I tempted Eric's flagging appetite until I found two things he would eat besides milk—small wheat crackers and peanut butter. As time went by, he increased the number of things he would eat; but his diet had remained extremely limited.

"And then there were the allergies," I said. For years as he was growing up he was constantly sneezing and blowing his nose. How could one small child blow with such high-decibel intensity, I had wondered. Sometimes when he had sneezed what seemed like twenty-five times in a row I would remember the verse in *Alice in Wonderland:*

> Speak roughly to your little boy
> And beat him when he sneezes.
> He only does it to annoy
> Because he knows it teases.[1]

I knew that Eric did not sneeze on purpose, but at times it was certainly annoying. Because I had impulses to speak roughly (beating was not even to be thought of) I became very guilty and very patient. The higher my irritation level, the calmer and more patient I became—outwardly.

Suddenly an idea that had been lurking in my mind took shape. "Aren't homosexuals supposed to be that way because of their mothers?" I asked Hans. "How could I help it? He demanded so much of my time and my energy. He didn't fit the usual patterns."

In his growing-up years he didn't fit the patterns either. He was always out of step. Perhaps if he had been less precocious . . .

"When he was five he should have been in kindergarten, but there was none in the school district where we lived," I said, resuming my thinking out loud. "In the morning he would watch *Captain Kangaroo.* The minute that show would be over, I would brace myself for the question, 'What shall I do?'

"We were living in the country, and there were no children his age living near us. If he wanted to play with anyone, I had to drive him there and back again. We had only one car, and if Tom needed it, which he often did, there went the playmates."

Eric's one joy for a long time had been inventing machinery made of Tinkertoys. The only drawback was that these inventions were very fragile, and the whole apparatus could suddenly collapse. Then there were loud tears of frustration from Eric and many internal tears of frustration for me.

I would sit down and patiently try to help him cope with frustration in spite of the fact that I wasn't coping very well myself.

My memories moved on. In the second, third, and fourth grades, Eric came home alone after school because all the boys were out playing baseball or football, and Eric didn't like sports. He was the Compleat Egghead.

He liked school and didn't care who knew it. This made him something of an oddity among the boys.

"Didn't Tom ever go out and play ball with Eric?" Hans asked.

"No, he really didn't. At one point I tried to talk Tom into giving Eric help with batting and catching, but Tom 'didn't have time,' and I don't think Eric really wanted to bother, even in order to have companionship. Maybe if Tom had come with enthusiasm and asked him . . . But he didn't.

"Eric always had one or two good boyfriends, however, until he was in eighth or ninth grade. At that point he had one friend, Andy. Suddenly Andy no longer came around. Eric was really hurt. He finally talked to Andy, who said no, he wasn't mad at

Eric—but that didn't change anything. Andy no longer came to supper or stayed overnight."

My heart had ached for Eric. He was doing extremely well in school, and he was beginning to find his own niche in extracurricular activities: art, band, dramatics, school newspaper. The teachers all liked him, and he was allowed to make his own "enrichment." He taught himself typing and shorthand. As he progressed through high school he picked up computer keypunching and a variety of other skills in his free hours. Even though he had no close friends, the kids seemed to like him and accept him as he was. He was not a recluse, and for that I was glad.

Through the years my heart ached for Eric for other reasons. From five or six years old on, when he climbed into bed at night and I would go in to say good night, he would ask, "Where's Dad?" Most of the time Tom was at church meetings. As time went on and we moved to Lakota, outside of Minneapolis, Tom acquired a study in the church, which was several miles from the parsonage. Then if he was not at a meeting, he was in the study at the church.

Sometimes I would feel angry with Eric. I wanted to shout, "You know where Dad is—he's at the church." Of course I didn't shout it. I would say it with the terrible patience that comes from beating one's head against a stone wall for years.

"Tell him to come in when he comes home," Eric would say.

It didn't matter what time Tom came home; Eric was almost always awake. Or he was dozing so lightly that Tom's whisper of Eric's name would rouse him.

"Did Tom ever relate well to Eric?" Hans wanted to know.

"Not really," I said. "He never was openly angry with Eric, but he could express displeasure about something in a way that just flattened Eric."

"You mean Tom would yell at him?" Hans asked incredulously.

"Goodness, no! You know Tom never raises his voice. It might have been better if he had. When he is really angry he has a way of expressing his displeasure quietly that is devastating. Poor Eric could hardly stand it. I would feel as if I had to do something to help him handle the pain Tom was causing him. It was usually out of proportion to what Eric had done."

"Still, when you were thinking you might move south to Mount Hope after the divorce, Eric wanted to stay with Tom, didn't he?"

I nodded. "In the end Tom postponed the divorce for some months so he wouldn't have to cope with Eric by himself."

As I said this I suddenly saw the whole situation from Eric's point of view. *His father had rejected him.* I had never thought of it that way before. Tom was hoping to get the divorce by the end of March, and I was scheduled to move to Mount Hope with Eric and Barbara. Emily was already a freshman at Trinity College there. Tom had rented a two-bedroom apartment in Lakota but had not yet moved into it. One night in February, Eric asked me if he could stay in Lakota with Tom until the end of the school year. I told Eric he could if Tom was willing.

Tom's answer was to postpone the divorce until after the school year was finished. By that time we had moved to a rented house in Lakota, and the whole plan for Eric, Barbara, and me to move south had fallen through. To me Tom's decision had been a reprieve. To Eric it had been rejection.

I remembered Tom's saying to Eric and Barbara, "You know I'm not divorcing you. I'm divorcing only your mother." But they hadn't known. His actions had said something different.

I remembered, too, Eric's loneliness for male companionship after Tom was gone and Eric was left alone with Barbara and me. "Take good care of Mom," Tom had said. "You're the man of the house now." Anger welled up in me now as I recalled this. Tom had not seen—he had never seen—how desperately Eric had needed him.

Hans interrupted my painful reverie. "How about a cup of tea?" he said, getting up and lighting the burner under the teakettle. "Then we can go sit in the living room."

It took a moment to refocus my thoughts. "Tea would be

fine," I said, while inside my heart was crying, "O my son Absalom, my son, my son Absalom! Would God I had died for thee, O Absalom, my son, my son!"[2] How strange, I thought. A father had once cried out those words, but I was a mother.

* * * *

When the tea was ready, Hans and I took our mugs and went into the living room.

"When Eric went to college I hoped he would find some real friends," I resumed after we were settled. "Maybe not many, but I thought there would be a few who would have interests and dreams that would parallel his."

When we had talked about college, Eric had made it clear that he didn't want to commute; he wanted his own apartment. I agreed that commuting was undesirable. Because of the distance involved, Eric's extracurricular activities would have been nonexistent. I wanted more from college for Eric than just book learning.

Neither could I picture Eric living in a college dormitory. It would be like trying to force a figure with all kinds of wild angles into a neat square or circle. There would be no possibility of making the two fit together. The solution seemed to be for Eric to have his own apartment and a part-time job. A scholarship took care of all tuition costs. With the job, a minimum of help from Tom, and a roommate with whom to halve rent and utility expenses, Eric could probably manage the apartment.

Eric put up signs at all the colleges in the area, advertising for a male apartment mate. These produced nothing more than some exploratory phone calls that brought no results. Finally Eric decided to pay ten dollars to a group that located apartment mates. This generated more phone calls but nothing solid.

The apartment expenses were getting heavy, and Eric finally advertised in the Sunday paper. He got quite a number of responses, and a few even came to see the apartment, but again, for some reason, nothing jelled.

I could see that beneath the surface there was a question in

Eric's mind: "Is this the way it normally is when you are looking for an apartment mate, or is it me?" I had the same question, and I didn't know the answer. I had no background of experience in this area with which to compare Eric's case.

At last he put up notices at some of the large industrial plants near his apartment, and finally a young man by the name of Bob moved in. I breathed easier.

It was a disaster almost from the first. Bob was a big hulk of a young man, nice looking, and accommodating in the manner of a huge friendly St. Bernard puppy. After the first month he had only to look at Eric with his St. Bernard puppy eyes to drive Eric right up the wall.

Actually I was surprised that Eric, with his definite tastes and his wild angles, didn't drive Bob up the wall. Perhaps, I thought, Bob was mercifully rather insensitive to personality clashes. I hoped so. Nevertheless, the situation bothered me. I hurt for Eric, but I hurt for Bob also.

Because I knew how much Eric needed Bob's help with the apartment finances, I tried to counsel Eric in ways to get along with Bob. "Wait..." "Try..." "See if you can't..." "Why don't you . . ." But there was no brooking Eric's feelings. He finally located another apartment mate and told Bob that a friend was going to move in with him. Bob simply shrugged, said, "OK," and moved out.

At first everything went swimmingly. Gregg, the new apartment mate, seemed like a real answer to prayer. The first hint of a problem came when Eric mentioned that Gregg was engaged, so he didn't know how much longer Gregg would be sharing the apartment, probably not after the end of the college year. Since this was early October, I was not too concerned. At least Eric was "covered" for the next nine months.

The next thing I knew, Gregg's wedding had been moved up to December. A week or two later I suddenly learned that Eric was alone again in the apartment. Even though the wedding was not going to take place for a month and a half, Gregg had moved into his fiancée's apartment.

"Hans," I said now, "did Gregg know anything about Eric, about his being a . . . a homosexual?" The word still didn't come out easily.

"Gregg certainly didn't know about it when he moved in," Hans answered.

"Did Eric ever . . . ask Gregg?"

"No," Hans answered. "But one of Eric's friends who came to the apartment propositioned Gregg. He was scared green. That was why he moved in with Diane even before the wedding."

After Gregg left, Eric had a couple other possible apartment sharers on the string. There was Mike, whose mother lived in Lakota. Somehow that fell through. Then there was Roger, whom Eric had wanted to take to Chicago at Thanksgiving time to visit Hans and Emily. That, too, had fallen through.

"That was a strange time for me," I told Hans. "Time after time in the evening when I would phone Eric's apartment he wasn't there. I had no idea where he was. For the first time in my life it seemed as if there were a wall between Eric and me. I knew that there was something on Eric's mind, but I didn't know what, and I didn't know how to ask him. I was glad that at least he had been able to talk to Henry Hilke in Mount Hope."

"Henry wasn't the only one Eric talked to," Hans said. "Henry suggested that when Eric got back to Minneapolis he should look up a counselor. Eric talked first with the chaplain at one of the hospitals, who referred him to Horace Brownell." He was a well-known pastoral counselor, affiliated with one of the largest churches in the Twin Cities. "Dr. Brownell had a number of sessions with Eric and helped him to feel more comfortable being gay."

Oh, he did? I thought indignantly. *Dr. Brownell helped him to feel* comfortable *being gay?* I was filled with wrath that any man of God should condone homosexuality. Why hadn't he tried to steer Eric away from it?

Hans was saying something about Gay Community Services. "Eric began going to meetings there and making friends. There are gay bars down around Hennepin and Fifth, and he began going there too."

So *that* was where Eric had been so often when I had phoned and no one had answered.

Summer had merged into fall, and Eric had begun his sophomore year at college. There had been some doubt in his mind about whether he would go back to college, but in the end he had decided he would.

In a rare talk with me that fall he said he felt much more at ease about himself. He didn't feel as much pressure as he had at one time. "I don't feel as if I have to run all the time and try to please other people," he said.

I don't have to run all the time. Literally he had run. I could always spot him at a distance or in a crowd. If the figure charged ahead full tilt, it was Eric. I had never realized before that he was running from himself.

College had been uphill all the way that fall. Not that he had trouble getting good marks. But for some reason college had simply lost its appeal.

When he had finally made the decision not to return to college after Christmas vacation, I had thought of it as "taking a leave of absence from college to see who he is." Now I suddenly saw that he had left simply because college was irrelevant to his new life. He was so busy finding and exploring the part of himself that had been hidden in the shadows for so many years that he had no energy to spare for absorbing other knowledge.

Hans was looking at his watch. "What about having some lunch," he was saying, "and then maybe you will want to take a nap."

Suddenly I realized how tired I was, how talked out. An hour of sleep, of rest, oblivion—how beautiful it would be!

"Yes," I said, "that's just what I need."

4

The
First
Step

A nap. How good it would have felt if I could have slept. I lay there on the sofa bed in the living room, my mind exhausted, my body weary, my eyes burning from lack of sleep. I wanted so desperately to sleep, but no sleep came. I turned the things we had talked of that morning over and over in my mind. And I prayed.

Hans had taken the Sunday paper into the bedroom to read. I kept hoping for his sake that he would fall asleep. But he didn't. The newspaper rustled regularly as he turned the pages.

As I lay there praying, ideas began to come. For some time—several months at least—I had been waking up more tired and tense than I had been when I went to bed. Sometimes I would feel as if I had a tight band around my head. Or I would have a lump in my throat, a pain in my back between my shoulder blades, or a sore muscle in my neck. During the day I could often consciously alleviate these nervous symptoms. Nighttime, when I should have been relaxed in sleep, was apparently the time of greatest tension.

And I dreamed. Sometimes I would wake up, conscious that I had been dreaming on and on and on for what seemed like hours. I knew that dreams performed a necessary psychological function, that people deprived of dreams for a long period of time could exhibit neurotic and even psychotic behavior. I reasoned that my mind was working overtime in sleep, trying to sort out my thoughts and feelings and to integrate them into my life. Judging by the number of aches and pains I had, my body was very much involved as well.

Some time before, my sister, Meg, had sent me Catherine Marshall's book *Something More*. The chapter "To Sleep, Perchance to Dream . . ." reminded me of the time, some years earlier, when my psychiatrist had suggested I write down my dreams and bring them to our sessions.

"It will help us know some of the things that are going on in your unconscious mind," he had said. For a while I had faithfully recorded my dreams.

Now as I became aware of my tenseness on waking and of the multitude of dreams tumbling helter-skelter through my mind during sleep, I decided that once again I might find help by recording my dreams. I bought a notebook and began writing them down.

In her chapter on dreams Catherine Marshall had included suggestions to help the reader interpret his or her dreams. With my notebook in one hand and *Something More* in the other, I would try to puzzle out what my dreams meant. I did not doubt for one minute that, crazy as they might seem, the dreams meant something. But no matter how hard I worked, how much I prayed about the dreams, or how much I asked the people in my dreams what they were doing there, I could not fathom what the dreams were telling me.

In the notes on that chapter Catherine Marshall had mentioned a book, *God, Dreams and Revelations*, by Morton Kelsey, an Episcopal priest who had served a parish in California for many years and who was now in the department of graduate studies at The University of Notre Dame. Perhaps this book could help me interpret my dreams. I bought a copy.

The book provided a great deal of information about dreams which I found tremendously interesting, but it did not give me the help I sought. Dream interpretation, it seemed, could not be done by rote from lists. One always had to take into account the dreamer's memories, the person's past experiences, and what was happening at the moment in that individual's life.

Now as I lay in Hans's and Emily's living room I began to think, if Eric is willing, perhaps he can be helped through his dreams. "Helped," of course, meant eventually cured of his homosexuality. I had no illusions that this would be easy. I knew that the percentage of cures was pitifully small. Still, some people made up that small percent. With prayer and the very best help available . . .

Who was the very best help? *Lord, to whom do you want to send Eric? Who is the very best help?* As I lay there, turning these questions over in my mind, Morton Kelsey's name occurred to me.

Yes! I thought. I had been thoroughly impressed with the soundness of his approach to dream interpretation in *God, Dreams and Revelations.* Even more reassuring, however, was a statement of his that Catherine Marshall had quoted in *Something More*:

> "First," he commented, "let's put any work with dreams in this framework. . . . The only way anyone should go into the unconscious is, first, to ask Jesus Christ for His power and direction and protection. Personally, I find that without Him I'm in danger even going to the grocery store without His direction, let alone trying to teach a college class."[1]

That's the man to whom I would entrust my son, I thought. He has the technical training and knowledge, as well as a direct personal relationship to Christ. That's the combination I want for Eric.

But Father Kelsey was in South Bend, Indiana, and Eric was in Minneapolis. Could we bridge that gap? Catherine Marshall had recorded her dreams, sent them to Father Kelsey, and set up a long-distance phone consultation. Suppose Eric were to fly to South Bend for an initial session with Father Kelsey. After that perhaps Eric could record his dreams, send copies to Father Kelsey, and have a phone conference with him periodically. I wondered if it would work.

"You're in Chicago," something said inside me. "South Bend isn't very far away. Why don't you phone and find out?"

I lay there a while longer. It took so much effort to sit up. At least, lying there, my body was resting even if my mind was active.

Finally, however, I became so restless that I got up. I padded into the kitchen to heat water for a cup of tea. Irrelevantly I remembered that travelers by dog team in Alaska drank tea, not coffee, when they were on the trail and needed endurance. Hans appeared almost immediately.

"You're up," he said. "Did you sleep?"

"No," I said, "did you? I was hoping you would."

"No," he said, "I've been reading the paper."

"I thought I ought to phone Eric and Barbara." We had talked of doing this earlier. I hesitated, then added, "I also think I will phone Morton Kelsey in South Bend." I explained the idea that had come to me while I was resting. It sounded a little farfetched as I told it to Hans.

"Surely there are good people in Minneapolis that Eric could go to," Hans said.

"I suppose so. But I want someone with a lot of know-how *and* a real deep Christian faith. The combination isn't always easy to come by."

"Perhaps Morton Kelsey could recommend someone in Minneapolis," Hans suggested.

"Perhaps," I said. Perhaps Tom would refuse to foot the bill too. I certainly didn't have money for prolonged treatment with Eric. *If it's what you want, Lord, you set it up,* I said silently.

Hans made tea for us both, and we went into the study.

First we phoned Barbara. The conversation did not take long. I told her that I knew about Eric now and that we would have to work out some rules about Eric's bringing friends to our house so that she would not be harassed again as she had been the night before. She did not say much, but she seemed a little more receptive to what I was saying than she customarily was.

Now we must call Eric. My hands were suddenly wet with perspiration, and my stomach churned sickeningly. I wanted to run, but I knew that I could not escape this moment.

"Shall I dial?" Hans asked.

"Oh, yes!" I said gratefully. At this crucial moment any help, no matter how small, was welcome.

Hans handed me the phone. I could hear the ringing and then Eric was saying, "Hello?"

"Eric, it's me, Mom. I'm in Chicago. I've just found out about your being . . . uh . . . about your being gay, and I just called to tell you . . . uh . . . that you are still my son. I won't disown you." The words sounded like a line from a bad play.

There was a long silence on the other end of the line. At last Eric said, "Well, now you know." His tone was bleak. There was another pause, and then he asked, "How did you find out? Did Hans tell you?"

"No, he didn't," I said quickly. "Barbara phoned at two o'clock this morning. She was pretty upset about your coming out to the house—"

"Oh," he said. "Yeah, I guess that was a pretty klutzy thing to do."

"I put two and two together. I asked Hans, and he never did say yes, but I guessed—I knew—"

"Yeah," he said slowly, "I suppose you would have guessed . . . Well, maybe it's good that you know . . ."

"We won't try to settle anything over the phone," I said, "but I just wanted to say I'm still your mother and I love you. We'll talk about it when I get back to Minneapolis. Hans wants to talk to you." I relinquished the phone thankfully. Why did my words sound so contrived? They were true.

Hans was talking to Eric. They were discussing the wisdom—or lack of it—that Eric had shown the evening before.

He seemed to have recovered from the initial shock of the phone call. There was an easy exchange between them that had not been there between Eric and me. Of course, Hans was Eric's brother-in-law, not his mother. They were also of the same generation. I belonged to a different generation, a different era.

Awakened by the word generation, a quotation suddenly came to mind: "Visiting the iniquity of the fathers upon the children to the third and the fourth generation. . . ."[2] The iniquity—or failures?—of fathers. And mothers . . .

Hans was going through the ritual of handing the phone back to me, and because I didn't know what else to say I gave a recap of what I had said before: "Just wanted you to know I know . . . still your mother . . . love you. I'll call when I get home, and we'll set up a time to talk." I laid the phone gratefully back on the cradle. It was done. It was over. Tears slid down my cheeks.

"Now that you know," Hans said, "maybe you will want to see a few of the letters Eric wrote to my dad last summer. He sent carbons to me."

"I don't want to violate any confidences," I said.

"Now that you know, I don't see how it could," Hans answered.

I took the papers he handed me. They were long letters, several typewritten pages each. As I read them I was aware that even in his personal letters, which were written at top speed, Eric had an artist's observing eye. From the letters I got the feel of Eric's discovery of himself. If only what he had discovered had been different. Perhaps—just perhaps—it could still be different.

That thought reminded me that I still had several phone calls to make. Hans left to go pick up Emily, and I phoned an airline to find out how much it would cost to get Eric from Minneapolis to South Bend and back.

Then, my heart beating faster, I called South Bend for Father Kelsey's number. And when I had it, I dialed.

A pleasant female voice answered. "Yes, he's here. Just a moment."

As simple as that. And then Father Kelsey was on the line. Yes, it was a possibility. Yes, it could be arranged. But I realized, did I not, that there was no guarantee of any specific results from all this?

Yes, I realized it, I answered. But one tried everything.

Somehow his voice was very comforting. The invisible man on the other end seemed to *know*. He knew what I was going through; he knew what Eric was going through. He did not take my side against Eric or Eric's side against me. He understood the dimensions of the dilemma. He knew that perhaps there was no answer as I might term an answer, but I felt no condemnation from him for doing what I had to do. Somehow the very quality of Father Kelsey's voice told me that here was a man who knew all about pain because he had seen it many times before. His voice came over the wire like a steadying hand in a dark place. There was no false hope in his voice, just a man looking at the reality of pain and helping me acknowledge it.

I hung up, a little dazed. It had been so easy. If you needed help, you just picked up a phone and called. *If it's right, Lord, you set it up*, I had prayed. And God had. The first step had been taken.

5

Battle
Plans

Why had it happened? How had it come about? As mile after mile vanished beneath the wheels of my car that Monday morning, the questions kept pounding over and over in my mind. They made a poor accompaniment to the overcast day and the mile upon mile of bleak snow-covered hills. Now and again a watery sunlight would break through the overcast, but it did nothing to lighten my mood or my thoughts.

I was on my way back to Minneapolis from Chicago. Before me stretched eight hours of almost trafficless freeway.

It was amazing to realize that less than seventy-two hours had passed since I was driving toward Chicago on this road. It seemed it must have been an eon ago. Life had changed irrevocably in those seventy-two hours. Actually (it took me a few minutes to make this calculation in my head), life had changed thirty-two hours before. It didn't seem possible. Already it seemed like a year.

Nothing would ever be the same again. No matter what happened with Eric, the fact that he was gay at one time in his life could never be changed. One could not deny that it had happened, whether he continued to be gay or not.

Words came to me unbidden from their hiding place in my memory. Eric had said after Hans's and Emily's wedding, "It made me sort of sad."

"Why?" I had asked.

"Because it will never be that way for me. It won't be in Mount Hope at Trinity Chapel. There's so much heritage in Mount Hope . . . It was just so beautiful . . . "

Within myself I had had to agree that since he would probably be married in his future wife's church, it was unlikely that Eric could duplicate the ceremony in Trinity Chapel. Unlikely, but not a total impossibility. Or so I had thought at the time. I had tried to express this to Eric.

Now I saw a totally different interpretation of his words: *It made me sort of sad.* Tears ran down my cheeks. It wasn't a question of persuading a girl to have the ceremony in Mount Hope. There was no girl, and there wouldn't be any ceremony. O God!

Where should I go, what should I do when wave after wave of intolerable pain washed over me? Especially when I was committed to eight hours of driving. I glanced at my watch. Two hours had passed. Six relentless hours still lay before me.

A year and a half before, when I had received word that Tom was going to marry Meta, the pain had been overwhelming. At that time a pastor friend had suggested what had seemed to me an odd approach: praise. For two years following the divorce I had prayed and hoped that we could be reunited. Up to that point there had always been the possibility of this, if not any real probability. Now that hope, that possibility, was finished. I had thrashed about like a wounded doe with a shaft straight into her heart but not yet dead.

Two couples had gotten together with me at my request for prayer. My intention had been that we should pray at that eleventh hour that Tom would be reunited with his family.

Instead, Gordon had brought with him a book, Merlin Carothers' *Power in Praise*, on which he had preached that very morning.[1]

"Mary," he had said rather hesitantly, "could I read you a couple things from the book?"

Everything within me had said, *"Praise? Now?"* And then some other wisdom had said, "You've tried everything else, and nothing has helped. Maybe a total annihilation of one's hopes demands something totally outlandish." That afternoon, out of obedience, I had said words of surrender and praise. I had gotten through the dreadful day of Tom's wedding on a wave of praise. In the year and a half since then I had come to a blank wall many times, and I had found that somehow or other when I turned to praising God a door would swing open.

Now as I drove I began to sing every hymn of praise that I knew. In the Community of the Resurrection, the church to which I belonged, we also often sang verses from the Bible set to music. When I had run out of hymns, I sang every scripture of praise that I could remember.

For two hours I sang as I drove through Wisconsin. For two hours I turned my back on the problem that blotted out everything else, and I looked at the one who had called himself the Way.

"Ah, Lord God," I sang, "behold, thou hast made heaven and earth by thy great power and outstretched arm; there is nothing too hard for thee."[2]

Something contracted in my heart, and suddenly there was a stillness and a peace within me. I thought of the words an angel had said to another woman in a quite different situation: "For with God nothing will be impossible."[3] A tiny seed of hope had been planted in my heart.

Now I began to settle down to some realistic thinking. Yesterday a fragment of a verse had come to me: "Visiting the iniquity of the fathers upon the children to the third and the fourth generation. . . ."

It was true. I knew that my mother's problems had been the cause of my problems. It seemed logical to suppose that in some way my problems were being passed on to my children.

Tom had problems also, though he refused to acknowledge them. Doubtless those problems had come to him from his parents, having been inherited from their parents. The problems went on and on, from one generation to the next.

And then I remembered the rest of the quotation: "to the third and the fourth generation of those who hate me, *but showing steadfast love to thousands of those who love me and keep my commandments.*"[4]

"I claim your promise of steadfast love, Lord," I said aloud, "because I do love you and I do try to keep your commandments, even if I often fail."

For with God nothing will be impossible. I felt an indefinable thrill go through me. What doors might God be waiting to open?

I knew intuitively that Eric was the way he was because of Tom and me, because of the climate of the home we had given him. None of our three children—Eric, Emily, or Barbara—had remained untouched. I knew that with certainty.

At the present moment, however, Eric seemed to have gotten the most obvious brunt of all that had been out of kilter between Tom and me. What I had read or heard about homosexuality (and it wasn't much) seemed always to connect it with a problem mother, a bad relationship some way or other between mother and son. A horrible domineering witch of a mother.

I knew I had not been that. If anything, I had been too soft, too overprotective. I hadn't meant to be. But there had seemed to be a great need to stand between Eric and all the difficulties that had assailed him, both physical and psychological. And Tom was too busy with the church . . .

As I drove now and sifted through the past years for insight and wisdom, I realized anew something I had seen years before: the pattern of one person in the marriage determined the pattern of the other person. The key determined the shape of the lock, and the lock determined the shape of the key. Which was designed first, the lock or the key? Which determined the design of the other?

The answer was that in some unconscious, totally instinctive way two people were drawn together because their crotchets, their hang-ups, meshed. The hills of one seemed to fit into the valleys of the other. I had seen it time and time again in my friends' marriages. After a while, those hills that fitted the valleys became the points of abrasion between the two. It had been so with Tom and me.

Eric and his problems—his Problem—had come out of his home environment. Was it possible, even at this late date, to do something about it? Suppose the three of us—Eric, Tom, and I—all had counseling. Could it swing the pendulum for Eric? It was too late to do anything about reuniting Tom and me, but if there could be changes in the way the three of us interacted, those changes might reduce the pressures on Eric and perhaps in time alter his orientation to life. His homosexual orientation.

I had no idea whether this was a valid supposition or not, but I felt that every last possibility was worth exploring. That meant that flying Eric down to South Bend was out. We would have to find someone in Minneapolis. When I got home I would write Father Kelsey and ask him to recommend someone.

I would also get in touch with Tom about the matter of money. The sooner the better.

It felt good to have some program of action, a plan to battle this hideous thing which had befallen our family. Maybe it was jumping up and down in one place, maybe it wasn't; but it was better than doing nothing.

I would also have to see Eric. Over the phone I had said, "We'll talk when I get back to Minneapolis." What was I going to say? What did I want to say?

I wanted to talk to him about counseling. I would also have to set up some rules about his coming to the house. For example, he was not to bring a friend out when I was not there. They could not be allowed to harass Barbara.

And when I was there? Could he bring a friend then?

Some of the old clichés arose before me. "Accept your children's friends. If you don't, you will not separate the children from the friends; you will only drive your children away from you." Did that hold good in a case like this? I didn't know.

How can a parent "accept" a child if the child is doing something that goes against every fiber of the parent's being? What does "accepting" a person mean? How do you accept someone when you disagree with him or her on a major point?

I tried another tack. Suppose I said to Eric, "You may come see me. You are welcome, but your friends aren't." Wasn't I saying, "Be something you aren't"? Was I pretending that what was real and true wasn't so?

On a more basic level, if I said that, would he ever come? Probably not. Did I want a growing distance between us? My heart squeezed painfully at the thought. "You are still my son" might have been trite, but it had said something real. Maybe others could close the door to their own flesh and blood. I could not.

But neither could I have them sleeping together under my roof. What they did at Eric's place was Eric's choice. Under my roof I had a choice. Suddenly I knew without any hesitation that they could come for a meal, but they could not sleep there. I didn't even want them kissing and putting their hands on each other in front of me.

Maybe I *wasn't* facing reality. Maybe I was pretending that what was real was not real, but I could not stand having them messing with each other in front of me.

These were the ground rules then: no coming to the house with a friend while I was not at home, no staying overnight with the friend, no displays of affection in front of me. Suddenly I understood Martin Luther when he had said, "Here I stand. I can do no other." It was as far as I could go in accepting—if indeed, this was any form of acceptance.

Now for the first time as I drove I allowed the full import of Eric's homosexuality to come over me—the sordidness, the danger. Particularly the danger.

I knew now from Hans and from Eric's letters which Hans had let me read that there was a bar downtown in Minneapolis—Ballard's—that Eric frequented.

Dear God, my son in a gay bar! I could see Eric among the strange-looking assortment. I had never been in a gay bar, but I could imagine what it might be like. There would be some young men like Eric, scrubbed looking and fresh. There would be some slightly older young men, neat and sharp looking, business types in casual clothes. It would go on down from there to longer hair, more untrimmed beards, hippier types. Some would be very handsome, with bold eyes; some would be in drag—I cringed at the thought—and some would be out-and-out freaks.

The freaks. The lacerated. The wounded. They would all be there. And Eric was there because he was one of them. Tears ran down my cheeks as I drove.

Ballard's was on Hennepin Avenue among the adult movie houses and bookstores, the rap parlors and the saunas, the pimps, the prostitutes. That was where Eric hung out. Where vice and violence were an accepted part of life.

Eric could easily be mugged down there on Hennepin Avenue. He could be raped. He could contract VD. He could end up in jail. (I wasn't sure just how, but it seemed a possibility.) He could be stabbed by a jealous lover. The whole gay world, I thought, lived much closer to violence than the straight world.

Two opposing worlds. I was part of one, and Eric was part of the other, and I wasn't at all sure that the twain could ever really meet. For my part I didn't want the two to meet. All I wanted to do was grab Eric out of that other world and run.

I became conscious that I must stop very soon for gas and that fine stray snowflakes were slanting in the wind which whipped across the highway. The sky had become a dull, opaque white, heavy with unshed snow.

As I pulled into a gas station I realized how exhausted I was. Two more hours to Lakota.

Suddenly I was nothing more than a tired child. "Dear God," I said, "please get me home safely."

I drove on through a world of falling snowflakes. Fortunately the persistent north wind drove the flakes across the highway. Those which did settle on the road surface were picked up and whirled about by every car that passed, but at least driving was not slippery.

I pushed on as rapidly as I dared. By the time I reached the east side of St. Paul the snow was lying heavy and treacherous on the freeways through the city. I gripped the wheel and plowed doggedly ahead, finding the lane as best I could.

"Hang in there," I said to myself. "You can make it. Only a few more miles. Hang on."

At last I was home. I set my suitcase inside the front door, put the car in the garage, peeled off my boots, staggered upstairs—coat and all—and flung myself on my bed.

I was utterly exhausted in mind, body, and spirit. But I was home. Safely. At the moment, that was all that mattered.

6

Tom and Meta

I awoke next morning with the residue of the previous day's exhaustion still clinging to me. For some moments I lay there, gathering strength to get up and face the tasks of the day. The night before, I had realized that I would be in no shape to keep my mind on work. And so I had phoned my employer and asked if I could work Wednesday, Thursday, and Friday of that week instead of Tuesday, Wednesday, and Friday. He had readily agreed.

Now as I lay there, thinking of those things which needed to be done that day, I felt a sudden need to know that God was with me, right at that moment.

"Give me a word, would you please, Lord?" I whispered.

I reached for my Bible and opened it at random. Isaiah 61 lay before me:

The Spirit of the Lord God is upon me, . . .
he has sent me to bind up the brokenhearted,
to proclaim liberty to the captives, . . .
to comfort all who mourn; . . .
to give them a garland instead of ashes,

41

the oil of gladness instead of mourning,
   the mantle of praise instead of a faint spirit;
that they may be called oaks of righteousness.[1]

I had underlined these words in my Bible long ago. My eyes went on now to words that had not been marked:

They shall build up the ancient ruins,
   they shall raise up the former devastations;
they shall repair the ruined cities,
   the devastations of many generations.[2]

My heart leaped. *They shall build up the ancient ruins, they shall raise up the former devastations; . . . the devastations of many generations.* The words were like a promise, like a ray of light just faintly visible above the black rim of hills as dawn begins to approach. In spite of my fatigue I felt a quickening of life. And I remembered the thought of the day before, *With God nothing will be impossible.*

"Thank you, Jesus," I whispered. "Oh, thank you."

The first duty of the day was to get in touch with Tom. I reached him at work.

"I found out this weekend about Eric," I said, "and I wondered if it would be possible for you and me to get together sometime today to talk about it. Could we meet somewhere for lunch?"

He already had a luncheon appointment.

"What about dinner?" I did not want to invite him to the house, and the only other alternative seemed to be a restaurant. It suddenly occurred to me that if money were involved, Meta would probably have to be included. All at once I found I didn't care if she was there or not. What did it matter? Whatever had once existed between Tom and me was dead. Our paths had gone in different directions. The only link we still had was the children, and one of those children was in desperate need. "If Meta wants to come too, that would be fine," I heard myself saying. "She's in this thing too."

"Not dinner," he said. "How about if we come to your place around seven?"

"I . . . I'd rather not," I said lamely.

"Why not?" he wanted to know.

I was silent. Tom had never been a part of this house. He had been in it very briefly once or twice, but it was mine, my sanctuary. I didn't want him looking around with speculative eyes and thinking, "Same messy housekeeper . . . Why doesn't she get some pictures hung? When is she going to get that sofa recovered?" and on and on.

"What's wrong with a restaurant?" I countered.

"It looks odd if someone sees us, and it's really not very private. Why can't we come to your place?"

I couldn't think of any good reason except the truth. "I—it's been my sanctuary, sort of. But I guess at this point those feelings are a luxury I can't afford. You and Meta come at seven."

"I thought it would be better than asking you to drive over to our place," he said.

To *their* place? God forbid!

"Yes, much better!" I replied. "I'll see you both at seven."

"All right," I said to myself after I hung up, "they're coming. There's nothing I can do to change that. I might as well make them feel at home."

What could I do to make the interview less difficult? A fire in the fireplace, of course. That had a warm, welcoming look. What about something to drink? Tea? Coffee? But that was a bother, a fuss. We had business to do, and I did not want to consume a lot of time making and serving. Yet I felt that a little oil of graciousness could ease what was basically an awkward situation.

Lord, help, I cried inwardly.

And then I thought of the half-full jug of cider in the refrigerator, left from the weekend spaghetti party. Hot mulled cider. It could be all ready. It did not need spoons, cream, lemon, or sugar, as tea and coffee did. My spirits lifted a little. It wasn't going to be so bad after all.

I went into the living room and began straightening it, collecting scattered newspapers, picking up dried fallen leaves from the plants, making a place in the closet for Barbara's skis, which had been leaning against the living room wall for weeks. There was no need to present my worst side. I would straighten the room, dust, and run the vacuum cleaner where it showed. The rest of the house might be a mess, but Tom need not know it.

I had two other tasks for the day that I felt were musts. One was to set up an appointment with Eric, and the other was to write to Father Kelsey to ask him for recommendations of possible counselors in Minneapolis or St. Paul.

Eric, when I reached him, said, "How about Thursday?"

"Fine," I said. "I'll come right from work. Why don't I pick up some food at the Burger Shack and bring it along for us?"

"Oh," he said, "are you going to be here that long?"

I supposed that if I were in his situation I might not be looking forward to a long interview with my mother either.

"I don't know how long I'll be there," I said, "but I don't function too well on an empty stomach." He gave me his food selection, and we hung up.

I sat down then and, after several false starts, drafted a letter to Father Kelsey. I finished it in time for the afternoon mail.

Barbara left at six-thirty that evening to play in the band at a school basketball game. Promptly at seven the doorbell rang, and I admitted Tom and Meta.

In a few minutes we were sitting in the living room talking, the initial stiffness eased by the business of hanging up coats and by the small ceremony of filling the waiting mugs with hot cider and serving them. The fire burned pleasantly on the hearth, giving its warmth and welcome.

I began with a brief summary of Barbara's early-morning phone call and went on to suggest that possibly Eric might be more open to counseling help if it involved Tom and me as well.

"Somewhere we got off base," I told Tom, "and Eric's trouble is the result. It may be too late for the counseling of all three of us to do any good, but then again it may not. If it would help, would you be willing? It seems to me we ought to leave no stone unturned."

Yes, Tom was willing. If it would help Eric, he was willing.

As we talked, part of me was standing to one side, observing the scene. In my wildest imaginings I could not have pictured such a meeting. Most of the dialogue went on between Tom and me, but as I talked I tried to include Meta in the conversation with my eyes, if not always with my words. Meta sat there, not looking at either of us, withdrawn into herself. I had the impression that if she had been able to press a button and cause herself to vanish, she would have. Once in a while when I looked and spoke in her direction she would come to life for a moment and be part of the group. Then she would immediately withdraw again into some private place.

I had a fleeting moment of pity for Meta. She was in a very uncomfortable spot.

"If there is counseling," I said, "it will cost money. I don't have the money for it. Would you see your way clear to it, Tom?"

He was silent, considering. It was a loaded situation, how loaded I had not realized until that moment. I was the past, reminding him of responsibilities he had assumed years before. Meta was the present. He had responsibilities to her as well. Each of us, simply by being there, was pressing her claim upon him. Each of our claims was legitimate, but undoubtedly they overlapped and collided.

At last Tom answered, "There's the insurance money for Eric's education. What good is it to save it for education if Eric is going down the drain?"

Together Tom and I had set aside that money years before to help finance the children's education. A third of it was earmarked for Eric. Tom had neatly sidestepped our conflicting claims.

"Do you have any ideas about whom to consult?" Tom wanted to know.

I explained about the direct route into the unconscious through dreams and said that I had written to Father Kelsey for recommendations of counselors in the area. He seemed to have no objection to this approach and offered no alternative suggestion.

At that point Barbara arrived from the basketball game. Meta brightened up and began an easy exchange with her about the outcome of the game. Tom had some questions about school. Our "meeting" was over.

They left very soon. As I watched them go I was filled with a melancholy surprise. Tom, the man I had once loved, was leaving my house with another woman, and I didn't care. As I watched them go I realized again that the love I had once had for him—or thought I had had for him—was gone.

But deep inside there was a sadness, an ache. For whom? For what? I didn't know.

I picked up the empty mugs in the living room. Tomorrow I had to go to work, step back into another world, and take my mind off the shattering events of the past few days. If I was going to function at all, I needed sleep.

7

Summit Conference

When I walked into the office the next day there seemed to be two of me. One was the outer Mary who said the usual things: "Good morning. Yes, I had a fine weekend." Dear God! That hardly described my visit to Chicago, but what else could I say?

There was also my inner self, who watched the outer self in disbelief. Over the weekend my world had fallen completely apart, but outwardly I typed letters from the dictating machine, checked inventory, took phone orders and messages. Outwardly I was behaving as usual, but inwardly I was still in a state of shock. Inwardly I was still lying in a heap saying, "It can't be." But, of course, it was.

Somehow seconds moved into minutes, minutes into hours, hours into days; and in the creeping inexorable way time has, two days passed and it was time to keep my appointment with Eric.

Again the disposing of my coat and boots and the business of dispensing food and drink eased the first difficult moments of our meeting. Eric had straightened and cleaned the living room till it shone. Somehow this seemed to indicate the gravity of the encounter. Summit conferences do not take place in messy rooms.

For a few minutes we were very busy eating, but the moment for which I had come could not be put off forever.

"Where shall we start?" I asked.

Fortunately Eric was not at a loss for words. "You remember that Wednesday before the wedding," he began, and he launched into the account of how he had talked first with Hans, then with Hans's father, then with Henry Hilke, and finally with counselors in Minneapolis.

"I wound up talking with Dr. Brownell, and he helped me to feel comfortable being gay. I've been going to a lot of meetings at Gay Community Services, and I have a lot of friends there."

I didn't know what to say. I wanted to be careful not to shut doors that I did not want shut, but I wasn't even sure what those doors were.

"Tell me more," I said.

"Being gay is really no different from being straight," he said, "except that you have all these feelings for a man instead of for a woman. It covers the whole bag—from a sort of marriage relationship to pickups and one-night stands.

"You know, when I was little, maybe five years old, I got the idea from you and Dad that sex with a woman was dirty, but you didn't say anything about sex with a man, so I thought that must be all right."

Dear God! I thought, startled almost speechless. *Five years old! What mother would tell her five-year-old son about not having sex with a man!*

Aloud I said, again groping for some sort of handle, "What is Ballard's like?" Ballard's was the only gay bar I could remember by name from Eric's letters to Hans's father.

"It's—well, you know what a bar is like?" He paused and looked at me. At another, less weighted moment I might have said, "I wasn't born yesterday." Now I only nodded. "Well, there's mostly men, but some women. Some of the women are lesbians, and some hang around because they like men but are afraid of them, and they know that with gay men they are safe."

"Are there many there in drag?" I asked.

"Some. Men in drag really turn me off. So do the effeminate ones. I like the really masculine ones. I see myself as masculine, and yet it's the masculine ones who appeal to me."

Once again, as had happened several times in the last few days, I felt as if I were two people. One Mary was talking quietly and listening attentively. The other Mary stood at a distance, observing the scene, trying to remember something. It seemed as if there was a piece of the puzzle just beyond reach.

"When did Tom find out about your being gay?" I asked.

"I told him last August. There didn't seem to be any reason not to. By August I was sure I was gay."

As he spoke I remembered last August. Up until then Tom had wanted Eric to accept Meta, but Eric had steadfastly refused. Tom had repeatedly asked Eric to dinner at his and Meta's apartment, but Eric had just as repeatedly refused. Somehow, despite the fact that Tom had some financial control over Eric, Eric had been able to hold out for luncheon meetings with Tom when Meta was absent.

One day Eric had casually mentioned to me that he had had dinner with Tom. Dinner? I had pricked up my ears.

"Just with Tom?" I had asked.

"No, Meta was there too."

An unpleasant suspicion that Tom had somehow tricked him crossed my mind. "Did you know Meta was going to be there?"

"Yeah," Eric had answered. "It was OK. I thought, if Dad's footing some of the bills, I can go along with his wanting me to accept Meta. It just didn't seem to matter to me anymore."

It just didn't seem to matter to me anymore. Suddenly I saw the progression. There was the little boy who asked nightly, "Where's Daddy?" *(Tell him to come in when he gets home.)* There was the adolescent boy whose father left him. *(I'm not divorcing you; I'm divorcing only your mother.)* That same adolescent boy was without male support in a completely feminine household.

(Take care of your mother. You're the man of the family now.) There was the young man who watched his father slip farther away as he married another woman.

And suddenly that young man had found a new world, the one he had been searching for, the place where a man—or men—loved him.

"I'm happier now than I've ever been before," Eric was saying. "Right now it's not really the sex that is so important; there hasn't been a whole lot of that. But it's the hugging and the kissing I like, and the friendship and love. These people operate on the same wavelength I do. I feel comfortable with them."

He became somewhat accusing then. I could feel a hostility in him that I had never felt before, even though it was carefully veiled. "You and Dad sure didn't prepare me for what real life is like," he said.

Careful, I said to myself. *Easy.* "In what ways did we not prepare you?" I tried to keep it a question asking for information, not a rhetorical defense.

"Oh, everything," he said. "You didn't teach me to dance—I love to dance. It's really great. I go down there and dance for hours. I love it."

"Who do you dance with?"

"The other men. We dance together."

"What else didn't we prepare you for?"

He was finding it difficult to explain. "Well, just the way most people live. You go down to Hennepin Avenue at night, and it's really alive. There are all kinds of people there. You"—his voice became faintly accusing—"you live some kind of life nobody else lives. At least you seem to be the only one who can make it work. You're sort of a religious fanatic, but most people aren't."

"You haven't met any others like me because you haven't gone where they are," I said, keeping my voice friendly. I thought he should know that there were others like me, but I was not interested at the moment in debating my religious fanaticism. He had just given me an opening I needed. "Eric, one of the things I am concerned about is the nightlife downtown. Maybe it looks great, but there is violence a lot closer to the surface than you are used to. It is pretty easy to get mugged and rolled."

"Oh," he said offhandedly, "I don't go into dark alleys or deserted streets. Hennepin is well patrolled at night by cops. I feel as safe there at night as I do in the daytime. Besides, I don't take any money with me when I go down there, just enough to buy a Coke, maybe. I don't go for the drinking. I like meeting people—friends—and dancing. Besides, I don't go to the bars that are dives."

"There's the problem of VD," I said. I felt he had to be aware of the hazards, and my guess was that Tom hadn't gone into any of this.

"That's no problem," he said airily.

"But it is," I persisted. "You can't always tell if the other person has VD or not."

"Mother!" he exclaimed as if I weren't very bright. "Maybe you can't tell with a woman, but with a man you can *see* if he has VD or not. Besides," he added easily, "if you should happen to pick it up, you just go get a shot and that takes care of it."

I sat there looking at him, and once again I could hardly believe that this was all happening. Part of me knew that this was real, but part of me was thinking: This is some kind of nightmare. This isn't the Eric I know. Did I raise him to be offhanded about VD, to love all the varieties of sin that flow along Hennepin Avenue at night? Dear God, was it for this that I spent nine months of waiting and eighteen years of child-rearing?

"Look, Mother," he was saying, "I have friends there. I'm not interested in the ones that are just looking for one-night stands. I want relationships that continue—friends—and I want a relationship like marriage with someone. There are all different levels in the gay world, just like in the straight world."

"How do you mean?" I asked weakly.

"I told you before. Some guys are just interested in one-night

51

stands. Others are looking for a longer-lasting relationship. Did you know that there are a lot of gay couples around?"

I shook my head.

"Well, there are. They live just like regular married couples. They aren't as interested in the bar scene lots of times; they just get together with other gay couples for their social life."

All at once I realized that I was exhausted. We sat in silence for a minute until I remembered that I had come for a purpose. Was this the right moment to offer help? How could I go about it gently and gracefully?

"Eric," I said, "this business of your being gay is—it's because of the situation in the home Tom and I made for you. I talked with Tom the other night, and if it would help for you to have counseling, he's willing. If it would do any good for someone to counsel the three of us—him and you and me—he's willing for that too."

"I was waiting for you to offer 'help,'" Eric said. "They always offer 'help' when they find out you're gay. It's the classic response."

Once again I avoided the challenge to defend my actions and continued, "I've been reading about using a person's dreams as the basis for counseling, and I thought that might be a more direct line into the unconscious than some other, slower means."

"I don't dream very much," Eric said. "Besides, I had so much counseling last summer that I just couldn't face any more digging around inside myself right now."

I remembered a time six or seven years earlier when I had felt exactly the same way. I could not urge him now, because I knew that what he said was the truth.

"I know what you mean," I said. "I understand. But both Tom and I want you to know that if you do want counseling, we're willing to help in any way we can."

He looked at me, and I felt again that carefully veiled hostility. "Why do parents always offer counseling?"

"Because if there's a chance of changing from homosexual to heterosexual, they want to offer it."

"But what's so much better about being heterosexual than being homosexual?" he asked. "There isn't one right pattern; there are a number of alternative patterns, and one isn't better than the other. Gay couples can live together for years and have respectable, decent lives, just like married people. In fact, gays should be allowed to marry. It's unfair discrimination that they can't—we're deprived of tax breaks, inheritance breaks, and a lot of things like that."

The part of me that was still able to be detached warned me, "Don't argue. You're getting the gay rights line, and at this point it is not really debatable in his mind."

"I suppose I see heterosexual marriage as the most complete type of relationship because it is able to produce a complete family," I said, praying that my tone was just neutral enough to be giving information rather than militantly planting a standard on a battleground.

Eric shrugged. "Maybe so. But I just don't get turned on by women, and I do by men. It's not something I decided on. It's something that just happened."

We sat for a minute in silence. I could think of nothing more that I wanted to say. I had come and I had seen, though I had not conquered.

"Why do you feel being gay is such a sin?" Eric asked after a minute or two had elapsed.

I thought for a moment, and something in me said, "Don't get snared."

I tried to choose my words carefully because I sensed that the future might hang on those words. "I think right now I can't go into the theology of it," I said slowly, picking my way cautiously. "The Bible has some statements about homosexuality, and for now I guess I have to say I go along with what the Bible says. I think you know that, and for me to try to pretend anything different would be false, and you would know it was false.

"You and I have very different attitudes about being gay," I went on, "but you are still my son, and I love you, and my door is always open to you." *Why do I always have to sound like a third-rate soap opera?* I wondered in the detached part of myself. *Why isn't there some way to say what one feels without its sounding nauseatingly corny?*

"However, there are a couple limitations," I added, remembering that I had not quite completed the agenda with which I had come. "You are welcome to bring your friends to my house, but you may do this only when I am going to be there. You're not to come or bring friends when only Barbara is there."

I wanted to go on and add that under no circumstances could he bring a friend to stay overnight; he could come alone and stay, but under my roof he could not sleep with a lover. But the words dried in my throat, and I thought, whether wisely or weakly, that these words could just as well be said when the necessity arose.

I looked at my watch and stood up. "I better go home and get some sleep so I can work tomorrow," I said.

"Would you take some pants of mine along to mend?" Eric asked.

Should I? Shouldn't I? What was he saying underneath? What would I be saying if I said yes? What would I be saying if I said no? I had at most thirty seconds in which to choose an answer on which might hang years of relationship.

"Sure," I said. "Which ones?"

He left the room and returned with four pairs. "This one needs some stitching here. This one needs the pocket mended. Can you mend this tear? And this one needs a new zipper."

I hated putting in new zippers. It was a tedious, fussy job. But I had said he was still my son. If I had to replace a zipper to prove it, I would replace the zipper.

"All right," I said. "Three of those won't take long, but it will take me a little time to do the zipper."

"And thanks," Eric said awkwardly, "for the supper and for offering—about the help. It's just that I don't need it now—I couldn't hack it." And then he said more smoothly and comfortably, "I've really never been happier than I am now."

I looked at him, and I knew it was so. It might not be perfection of relationship, but it was better than anything he had known for a long, long time, probably since his one best friend in eighth grade had opted out of the relationship.

"I know," I said as I struggled into my coat and put on my boots.

"I don't dream much," he said, as if we had just been talking about it. "The only dream I can remember recently was about a whole lot of numbers and letters—I suppose because I was using them in a line of graphics the other day."

"Yes," I said. "It's OK. It was just an offer if you wanted it. I'll work on the pants."

"Thanks for coming."

"I'll be talking to you." I turned and went down the stairs. Behind me I heard the door shut.

At home I hunted up *God, Dreams and Revelations*. Eric didn't know it, but he had given me a glimpse inside his head when he told me about the dream of the letters and numbers.

I found the right page and read:

These dreams suggest that an individual's conscious attitude is "adequate" toward the psychic forces within him; it takes in enough of the unconscious to be in balance with it, at least for the moment. These dreams are very often abstract; they deal with images and figures that symbolize the complex situation within the person, but they often stress form and relationship by putting the emphasis on geometric, numerical, or even color arrangements.[1]

"These dreams suggest that an individual's conscious attitude is adequate' toward the psychic forces within him; it takes in enough of the unconscious to be in balance with it, at least for the moment."

Eric had put it in his own terms: "Thanks for offering—about the help. It's just that I don't need it now. I've really never been happier."

There seemed to be only one avenue left to me. I had hoped that Eric would accept counseling. If he had accepted it, the way might have been opened for Tom and me to receive counseling also. I had so hoped that there was a possibility of repairing some of the damage to all three of our children that Tom and I had inflicted over the years. It was not to be. Unless . . .

Unless I offered myself. I had visualized three channels. But I had control over only one channel—myself. It was time to get down to business. If there was only one gate into the situation, then I would use the one gate.

In my notebook journal I wrote, "Because there is no other way to break into the problems, I offer myself. Deal with me, Lord, so that I shall be different and therefore have a different relationship—more healing and helping—with them."

8

Eric's "Friend"

When I answered the phone that first Monday evening in March, Eric was on the other end of the line.

"Hi, Mom. What are you doing Sunday?" he asked. He wasn't one to dally in small talk. "If you're not busy, I was wondering if we could come to dinner."

We. I was going to meet Eric's "friend."

I could feel the primitive reaction of my body to attack. It manifested itself in the sudden pounding of my heart, in a sudden trembling of my hands. But as I answered I strove to keep my voice normal.

"I'm not doing anything special," I said. "That would be fine."

"Did you understand what I said, Mom?" Eric asked. "I said, could *we* come to dinner?"

"Yes, Eric, I heard. Who are you bringing?"

"Brian," Eric answered. He didn't say it, but his tone added, "of course." I knew that Brian had moved into the apartment with him.

"Brian and I are coming up to church at Lakota, so I thought it would be a good time for us to come to dinner," Eric said. I interpreted this to mean, "It would be a good time for you to meet Brian."

"Church is over around twelve," I said. "Shall we figure on twelve-thirty?" It was settled, and we hung up.

My knees felt weak as I got up and walked away from the phone.

"You are welcome to come up anytime," I had said, "and you are welcome to bring your friends." How easy it was to say those formula words, but now that I was faced with impending reality I wondered if I could go through with it. What had I let myself in for?

I wondered also if I was really doing the right thing. A quotation from the Bible rose before me: "What fellowship has light with darkness?"[1] It seemed to me that homosexuality was very great darkness.

Soon after I had learned about Eric, I had gone to talk with Paul Sundstrom, the pastor at the Community of the Resurrection.

"You can't help a person who is homosexual unless he wants to be helped," Paul said.

"I know that," I answered. "But is there anything a parent can do spiritually that will help?" I knew that things had a way of filtering down from the spiritual world into the physical.

Paul considered that for a few minutes, waiting, I knew, for the Lord's guidance.

"There are six things you can do," he said at last. I had brought along a pad of paper to take down any instructions, and I reached for it now.

"First," he said, "make sure that the relationship between God and yourself is right. Make confession of any unconfessed sin.

"Next, Jesus has broken the power of every curse—and homosexuality is a curse—but you know Jesus has broken the power of that curse because it says so in Galatians 3:13." He turned the pages of the Bible on the desk in front of him and read, "Christ redeemed us from the curse of the law, having become a curse for us—for it is written, 'Cursed be every one who hangs on a tree.'

"Third, you can pray that the Lord will break into the vicious cycle repeating through the generations." I had told him how both Tom and I had been damaged by our parents, who, through circumstances, had been damaged by their parents, and so on, probably, back through generations we didn't even know about.

"Fourth, he gives the light of the glorious gospel for this. That reference is given in 2 Corinthians 4:4.

"Fifth, homosexuality is always a spirit because it is an unnatural form of behavior.

"And sixth, as a parent you can rebuke that spirit in the name of Jesus. No one can cast out a spirit from a person unless he wants the spirit cast out, but you can rebuke that spirit in the name of Jesus."

I wasn't sure what the difference was between rebuking a spirit and casting it out, but I felt sure that Paul knew. He prayed then, taking up each point that he had outlined, claiming those promises from the Bible which he had given and rebuking, as the pastor of Eric's mother, the spirit of homosexuality in Eric.

The interview was fine as far as it had gone, but it didn't give me any guidance concerning entertaining Eric and Brian at dinner. Was I really condoning their sin, perhaps even encouraging them in it, by inviting them to dinner? I had thought it would be all right for Eric to bring his "friend" home, but now I wasn't so sure.

It was probably an indication of the tension within me that I called three different people that week for help. Paul Sundstrom was busy, so I talked with Fred Kreitzman, one of the elders. He had some doubts about the undertaking, but he felt that since I had already agreed to the dinner I had better go ahead with it.

Meribel Justeson, a friend from the Community of the Resurrection, was more positive. A mother herself, she understood that mothers are apt to yearn for their children, particularly straying ones. We prayed silently for a few minutes, and then she said, "Mary, as we prayed it came to me that in the Spirit you are beholding God with awe and reverence. You are seeing the magnitude and power of God's love, and therefore you can eagerly expect God to do a new thing in this situation. Therefore you can praise God for this opportunity, even though you don't know what the Almighty is going to do. God wants to be revealed more and more in this situation—to show you new dimensions of what God is like."

It was a heartening thought.

The third person I talked to was the director of a Christian live-in house for people with emotional problems. He was extremely dubious about the venture. In fact, he recommended that I cancel the dinner.

It was now Friday evening, and they were coming Sunday. As I was driving home from a meeting I began talking to the Lord.

"Jesus, they're coming Sunday. Whether it is right or not, I haven't had the courage to call up and say, 'Don't come.' How shall I deal with this? What do you want me to do?" And again, as I often had in the past, I asked, "Lord, give me a scripture verse to guide me."

Suddenly I remembered some verses in the Bible about Jesus' eating with sinners. As soon as I got home I bounded up the steps to my bedroom and grabbed my small concordance to locate the reference. In a few minutes I had a number of verses. Some of them were references to the same story in various Gospels, but I remembered a biblical scholar once said that when a story appeared in three or four Gospels, God was in reality saying, "This one is especially important. Pay attention."

I checked several verses in Matthew and Mark. When I got to the fifteenth chapter of Luke, I knew I had my answer. The whole chapter talked not about shutting the door on sinners but on reaching out with love.

That was it, I thought in sudden excitement. The keynote of the dinner Sunday was to be love—not my love, because I doubted that I had any, but God's love.

"How do I show your love?" I asked.

The oldest and simplest way seemed to be to serve what I knew Eric would like: steak, hot rolls, corn, carrot and celery sticks, and chocolate cake for dessert. The menu popped into my head full-blown. It was hardly a gourmet meal, but then I was not cooking for a gourmet.

Eric and Brian had planned to go to church in Lakota and come to my house afterward. At twelve o'clock Sunday the phone rang. It was Eric.

"Uh, we overslept and didn't get to church. In fact, we just woke up. So it will be awhile before we get there. Would one-thirty be all right?"

"That would be fine," I said. I hadn't planned to do the steaks until they got there, the corn and rolls would take only fifteen minutes, and the rest was ready.

At one-thirty the phone rang again. "We're just leaving now," Eric said. "Is that OK?"

"Yes, that's OK," I said, reaching over to the stove and turning off the heat under the corn. It would probably take them forty minutes to reach Lakota.

Whatever the reason, it took them a full hour to arrive. The two-hour wait had done nothing to calm my nervousness.

I was unprepared for the fact that Brian was considerably older than Eric. Older not only in years—Brian was twenty-eight to Eric's nineteen—but in sophistication as well. He was attractive in a bold, blond, Viking way. With a horned helmet and a leather shield he could have swashbuckled his way through any adventure movie.

It was not the worst of afternoons, after its slow start, nor was it the best of afternoons either. It was more like some initiation rite that had to be completed. We were all very dutiful about being polite, making conversation, and passing food.

"Would my smoking bother you?"

"Not at all." A polite lie. The house would reek for a day afterward. "Eric, would you find Brian an ashtray?"

"The steak is very good."

"I like this chocolate frosting."

"Where do you work? I see."

"How is it going at work, Eric?"

Small talk. Very small.

After dinner we went into the living room. I lit a fire in the fireplace, but I had trouble getting the wood to burn. We all worked at it, checking to see that the damper was open, rolling up newspapers and stuffing them under the logs, opening the front door in hope of creating a draft up the chimney. It gave us something to do (thank God!). It filled time.

We talked. Brian yawned. We talked. Brian yawned some more. He apologized and said he didn't know why he was so tired. I couldn't tell him that I was tired, too, from the psychic ordeal we were all undergoing.

About five-thirty he and Eric went out to the garage to change the oil in Eric's car. I was utterly wrung out and exhausted. At last the oil was changed; it seemed to take forever.

Then a few more polite words. "How about a bite of supper?"

"Thank you, I'm still full from that good dinner."

"I think we have to be going along."

"Thanks so much for having us."

"It was so nice to meet you."

And they were gone. I was so exhausted I didn't know what to do. I tottered back into the living room and collapsed into a chair, tears running down my cheeks.

"O God," I said. "O God, O God, O God." I felt as if I were a thousand years old. As if an army of tanks had pounded over my body. As if I had been stretched on a rack since the dawn of time. As if I could never again think or feel or ever, ever smile again.

I had no idea anymore about showing God's love or expecting God to do a new thing in this situation. I didn't care if I ever discovered new dimensions of what God was like; as Meribel had said. All I asked from the Lord at that point was the energy to clean up the kitchen and crawl upstairs to bed because, unfortunately, tomorrow was another day.

9

Lee

The ordeal was over. I had done it. Eric and Brian had come to dinner, and I had survived.

It took me several days to recover from the emotional exhaustion of the encounter. In the back of my mind I knew that sometime I would probably have them to dinner again, but I couldn't even let myself think about that now. I could only trust that when the time came, the Lord would give me the necessary fortitude and grace. Meanwhile there was a much more pressing problem to be dealt with. Morning after morning I was waking with the familiar aching neck, aching shoulder blades, aching head, and lump in my throat.

For more than a year, every time there had been a healing service at the Community of the Resurrection, every time anyone had asked, "Does anybody want prayer for healing?" I had gone forward. I had lost count of the times I had had prayer for the healing of my high blood pressure and more recently also for the relief of tension. I prayed constantly for these healings, but nothing happened. It had begun to dawn on me that perhaps God was choosing to heal me in some other fashion.

I knew, of course, that I could take tranquilizers in order to relax. This was only a stopgap measure, however, and I preferred to avoid it if at all possible. I had had experience with tranquilizers, and though at times I had been exceedingly grateful for them, they were certainly not the cure I longed for.

Since prolonged prayer had not brought the spiritual healing I had sought, it seemed as if the only other course of action open to me was to find out what was going on in my unconscious and to give it a thorough housecleaning. For this I knew I would need help, probably much more help than any of the counselors at the Community of the Resurrection was trained to give. It would probably also require more time than anyone on that staff was able to spare.

The problem in finding a psychiatrist or a psychologist was that I wanted a well-qualified *Christian* counselor. It was not easy to find thorough training combined with thorough Christian commitment.

In reply to my letter asking him to recommend possible counselors in the Minneapolis area, Father Kelsey had sent only one name: "Ms. Lee Lundquist . . . young (about thirty) with a degree in social work and a marvelous Christian and psychological background. I can recommend her without qualification."

A woman. Among all the counselors I had seen through the years, I had never had a woman. Suddenly I thought, "I believe I might be better able to talk to a woman."

I phoned Ms. Lundquist and made an appointment.

The whole setup with Lee Lundquist was different from any previous counseling situation I had been in. She did not have an office. Instead, I went to her home, where she had a small room in the walk-out basement fitted up for a consulting room. It was paneled, with floor-to-ceiling bookshelves; an oriental rug on the floor; two comfortable, slightly worn chairs; and a small table. There were various small posters on the wall, several stained-glass suncatchers hanging in the window, and many plants. It was a warm and inviting room.

Lee was open and friendly. She had short, curly, light-brown hair and brown eyes and was casually dressed in slacks and several layers of sweaters.

In that first session Lee and I talked about the most recent dream I had written down. After two months of recording my dreams in a notebook, I had accumulated a good-sized collection. But they might as well have been written in Sanskrit or Chinese; I could interpret none of them.

It was fascinating to see her take a dream that had been totally opaque to me and help me "see into" it. She did not interpret it for me, but through questions that she threw out, analogies from mythology, insights from Jung and other psychiatrists, she provided an entrance into the mystery. I could hardly wait for the next appointment. With a few more sessions like that, I felt, I would soon be able to interpret my own dreams.

* * * *

The second time Eric and Brian came to dinner, things went much better than they had the first time. I had learned in the meantime that there was no need to talk of Sunday dinner before two o'clock. Their sleeping and waking patterns over a weekend might be topsy-turvy according to middle-aged thinking, but by setting dinner for a realistic time I stood a better chance of their arriving at the specified hour. It also meant I didn't have to miss church on the days when they were dinner guests.

Barbara usually worked from 2:00 P.M. to 9:00 P.M. on Sundays, an arrangement that allowed her to absent herself while they were there and thus lessen the tension for everyone.

This time all three of us were much more relaxed. Eric's and Brian's prompt arrival helped considerably. As the afternoon progressed, Brian exhibited none of the yawns and sleepiness that had beset him on the first visit. In fact, he seemed to enjoy himself very much. After a leisurely dinner, we read the Sunday papers and followed that with several games of cutthroat Parcheesi. By that time we were all hungry again.

"We'll fix supper for you," Eric offered when I suggested getting something to eat. "How about my scrambling some eggs? And Brian can make pancakes."

I accepted their offer. While they turned the small kitchen

65

upside down with their cooking, I puttered about, setting the table, telling them where to find the right-size bowl, pouring milk, and making coffee.

It was after eleven when they left. I felt the satisfaction of a hostess who has given a good party. They certainly must have enjoyed it, or they would not have stayed so late.

As I rinsed plates, put them into the dishwasher, and wiped the counters and stove, I thought about the day. And as I thought I became aware of a great sense of lightness, almost of relief. I had watched Brian and Eric as they related to each other, and as I watched I began little by little to realize that my burden with Eric had been lifted. Somehow I no longer needed to feel responsible—for raising him, for trying to insure his happiness, for standing between him and the pains and blows of life. Brian had taken this over.

Ever since Andy had faded out of the picture I had sensed Eric's loneliness, Eric's searching for . . . what? I hadn't known, but I had sensed his need. And because I had been conditioned by life to try to fill the needs of others, I had striven to respond.

It was as if he had continually been holding out a cup to me, asking silently that I fill it with something to quench his thirst. And I had poured, and poured, and poured, but what I had poured had somehow been unable to quench that thirst. Did it spill outside the cup? Or did I go through the motions of pouring when I was so dry inside that nothing was coming? Or was what I poured unable to quench his thirst because I did not have what he was thirsting for?

I understood now what it was Eric had wanted: friends, companionship, a father to relate to him, and ultimately a wife and marriage. And in a strange, reverse way, like the negative of a photograph, Eric now had all those things. At last he was part of a community—the gay community—and in Brian he had father, friend, companion, wife, and marriage.

And I felt guilty, even as I felt relieved. Eric had found something he was looking for, and it relieved me of a burden I had been carrying, and I was glad and light and happy and free. Except. Except that he had found all this in a sinful way of life.

How in the world could I be relieved and rejoice in that? So I was glad, and I felt guilty because I was glad.

I could hardly wait for my appointment that week with Lee. "It's the strangest thing," I told her. "I don't understand it, and I know it's a wrong and sinful relationship, but I can't help being glad Eric has found Brian. It has taken such a load off my shoulders.

"Do you know he's training Eric to eat a lot of things he would never touch before?" I rushed on. "Eric ate those scrambled eggs on Sunday night, and they apparently have cheese omelets frequently. He never ate cheese before this, either. He's eating pizza, and he has tried shrimp. It's amazing!

"And Brian is working on Eric's table manners and other annoying things that I never made any headway with at all. Eric doesn't always listen to him either, but Brian is getting a lot farther with him than I ever did, and I just feel as if a great burden had rolled off my shoulders.

"It's such a peculiar relationship," I went on. "Brian is nine years older than Eric. In some ways Eric is very mature, but in some ways he's very naive. I really don't understand their attraction for each other.

"Apparently Brian is the wife and Eric is the husband. I would think it would be the other way around because Brian is older. Actually neither one of them looks or acts feminine. It's very strange. I must be out of my skull, but right now I really don't want anything else for Eric."

Lee smiled. "It sounds as if that was a good encounter with Eric and Brian," she said. "They have something good going for them, and you have a good relationship with them. You are out from under a burden and perhaps have a chance to look around and take stock. That's kind of neat."

I left with a slight spring in my step. Perhaps I had not flipped as completely as I had thought.

*   *   *   *

As spring moved into summer, I began to hope that the counseling would soon be over. I was very conscious of the money going out and not coming back. Besides, the aches and pains I had had were much better. "There can't have been that much wrong with me," I thought. "A couple of months' counseling should do it. I wonder when I can quit."

In addition, Lee's and my times together were often painful. I wondered if it made sense to pay money to rake through dead ashes and find only pain. I knew I did not want the chemical painkillers. What I wanted was some kind of psychic formula or prescription to take away the pain. This Lee would not give me. Or could not.

Once, at the end of a particularly painful session when I had done almost nothing but sit and weep, hardly even knowing why I wept, I had asked her, "What can I *do*? Isn't there some way to avoid so much pain? Can't *you* do anything? Aren't there ways?"

She had sat silently with me while I wept. There was a look in her eyes I could not interpret—almost, I would have said, a recognition of pain and an acceptance of that pain. Now and then she would break the silence and ask, quietly and gently, "What are the tears? What are they saying?"

But I did not know what they were saying. They came from some deep well inside myself, and they brought with them so much pain that it was agony and anguish. But what they were saying I did not know. All I knew was that I wanted this cup to pass from me. I did not want to drink the pain presented to me.

She looked at me with those eyes which knew and recognized pain, and she said in answer to my questions, "All you can do is feel the pain. Give it a place in your life."

"But I don't want to," I said. "I want it to go away. For good."

"You don't have to dwell in pain all the time," she said in her quiet way. "You can set a limit to it. It doesn't have to take you over. But to give it no place at all means only that then it will demand too much of a place. It will stake out its claim without regard to your wishes."

"Can't I avoid it?" I cried in desperation. I hurt so very, very badly inside.

And she said, "Pain is part of life. No prince or princess ever lives completely happily ever after."

I looked at her for a long time, and she looked steadily back at me. So that was it. I had been a child, crying for an impossible moon. It was not possible to avoid pain completely. That day I knew I had touched truth.

There were good sessions, too, after which I would find that I had energy enough to accomplish many tasks at home that needed to be done.

After one of these good sessions I would think that perhaps I could taper off on the counseling. I was still very skittish about it.

"Maybe I could get along with seeing you only once every two weeks," I said to Lee one day. "Maybe I don't need as much therapy now."

But Lee knew better than I that we had barely dug to the first level.

"You are on a pilgrimage," she said. "You are searching for answers. I can't give you the answers because I don't have your answers. *You* have to find them. But I can walk with you as you explore. Sometimes we need somebody who is willing to walk with us. It's not as scary as when we are alone."

I yielded to what she said and soon discovered how right she was. First Lee went on vacation. Shortly after she returned, I took my vacation. And I found that without those hours when I could go and delve into my depths, all my physical pains returned. I was right back where I had started.

I did not really have a choice as to whether or not I would see Lee.

10

Glimpses
Beneath the
Surface

One Sunday in early October, I hurried home from church to set the table and put the finishing touches on a company meal. Eric and Brian were coming to dinner.

The phone rang. Meribel Justeson was calling to ask if I would play the organ for a funeral on Tuesday for the sixteen-year-old victim of a hit-and-run accident.

I hadn't touched an organ in five years and would gladly have said no except that there didn't seem to be anyone else at the Community of the Resurrection who could play the organ. (Because our building was still unfinished, we used a piano for services.) I was willing to help, however, if I was really needed.

"Meribel," I said, aware that my dinner guests would soon be arriving, "if you can possibly find someone else to play, please do. If you can't, call me back and I'll do what I can."

Eric and Brian arrived, and dinner and the rest of the afternoon passed pleasantly. It wasn't until around nine o'clock, just as we were finishing supper, that the phone rang.

"Are you still willing to play for the funeral on Tuesday?" Meribel asked. "I couldn't find anyone else."

"All right," I said, "I'll play. Did they mention any favorite hymns?"

"No," Meribel answered. "But they did say they wanted hymns that were not real joyous, but not sad either."

"I'll start hunting for some right away," I said, and we hung up.

Eric and Brian were planning to leave for Ballard's right after supper. I asked if they would mind if I began going through the hymnbook while they finished their meal. I didn't have a whole lot of time to prepare because I had to work the next day, and by evening I would probably be too tired.

I had expected them to finish supper and leave for Ballard's at once. To my surprise, as I began going through the hymnbook, jotting down suitable hymns, Brian and Eric began to enter into the selection with me. We discussed word content (though the hymns would only be played, not sung) and music.

Before I knew it, I was at the piano, and for two hours I played hymn after hymn, and we sang. At intervals Eric would remind Brian that they wanted to get to Ballard's, and Brian would say that there was still plenty of time. Then he would say, "Play this one," and we would be off again.

At last Eric said rather urgently that if they didn't leave now, they wouldn't even get to Ballard's before it closed.

Brian shrugged. "So what if we don't?" he said and set the hymnbook in front of me, open at another hymn.

It was close to eleven-thirty when they left.

As the door closed behind them, I sank into the big chair in the living room, speechless. The kitchen needed straightening before I could go to bed, but I had to think.

Brian, suave and sophisticated (at least that was the impression I had had of him), had chosen two hours of playing and singing hymns rather than two hours at a gay bar. I was amazed that he would choose such a simple, homespun activity in preference to what I supposed was "his type of fun." It had been a scene out of a vanished era, a mother playing hymns on a Sunday evening for her family. A mother . . .

Who was Brian's mother? Where was she? Who was his father? Where was he? He never mentioned either of them. He had a grandmother whom he referred to as Viola. She seemed to be a rather gloomy, querulous old woman. Apparently his grandfather had died several years previously.

He also talked about an aunt and uncle, Florence and Herman, who had bad tempers and spent quite a bit of time fighting. But mother and father? He did not speak of them.

At last I rose from the chair and began putting plates and glasses into the dishwasher. I had no answer to the riddle, but I felt that I had had an unexpected glimpse of a different Brian.

Many months later I learned from Eric that Brian was born out of wedlock. Sometime after his birth, his mother had married and moved to Florida, leaving him in the care of her parents, who raised him. Eric reported that now and again he would see his mother if she happened to be coming to Minnesota, which wasn't often, I gathered. His father was in Montana. Brian saw even less of him than of his mother.

Later I was given further glimpses beneath the surface of what I referred to in my thoughts as "the homosexual world." I was at Eric's apartment, typing my annual Christmas letter, which was to be printed and included with my Christmas cards. Eric had offered the use of his typewriter because it made a better-looking copy than mine.

Brian was there, having missed work because he had overslept. He offered me coffee, showed me the intricacies of the typewriter, and, as he said jokingly, generally tried to be "a good hostess."

Not host. Hostess. How strange, I thought again, that a man who looked so swashbucklingly masculine should see himself in a woman's role.

I had finished my typing and was standing in the living room talking with Brian for a moment before leaving when my eye fell on a framed poem hanging on the wall.

I moved closer and read it. The poem spoke movingly of the

72

despair of a young gay man leaving a bar alone at closing -
going home to the loneliness of an unshared bed.

"Who wrote it?" I asked, swallowing the lump which had
risen in my throat as I read.

"Dan wrote it, and Eric designed the layout," Brian answered. Dan, I knew, was one of their friends.

For a moment I stood, impaled by the message of pain the
poem conveyed. After twenty years of marriage and a double
bed, I knew intimately the pain of loneliness in the night. Dan
was talking about a totally different situation, but was his pain
so different from mine? His being gay did not make his pain any
less real or intense. Though we had each dealt with our loneliness by widely divergent means, I understood what he was
saying.

Shaking off my reverie, I turned to go. "Thanks for the coffee,
Brian, and tell Eric I thank him for letting me use his
typewriter."

Once in my car and speeding along the freeway, I thought
about Dan's poem. I had always looked down somewhat from
my little pinnacle of goodness on those who frequented bars or
sought casual sex.

Now I saw that in my self-righteousness ("God, I thank thee
that I am not like other men."[1]) I had condemned people and
their actions without being aware of their hidden moti-
vations—of the hidden pain that often drove them.

As I drove I wept for the pain of a young man I didn't even
know. At one time I would have said, "What else can he expect
except pain when he lives the sinful life of a homosexual?"

Now I was not nearly so sure of what was cause and what was
effect. I was beginning to see that perhaps those things which
seemed so sinful to me—the endless searching for casual sexual
contacts as well as the ongoing relationships such as Eric and
Brian had—had been chosen more out of a desperate need than
because the person willfully wanted to sin.

"Forgive me, Lord," I murmured, keeping my eyes on the
road as I felt in my purse for a handkerchief. "I didn't know. I
just didn't know."

73

11

No Easy
Answers

Soon after the beginning of the new year, I received a clipping in a letter from my sister, Meg. The clipping was a letter from the magazine section of *The New York Times*, written by a New York psychiatrist and author, Irving Bieber. He was replying to an earlier article that had made misstatements concerning his work.

As I skimmed the clipping, certain phrases caught my eye:

A research team of ten, including myself, found that the fathers [of male homosexuals] were mostly detached and hostile, not absent.... Not one subject had had a loving, constructive father. ... Over the past twelve years I have personally interviewed more than 900 homosexual men, and all the information gathered continues to support our original findings.... I have concluded that given a good father-son relationship no boy develops a homosexual pattern.[1]

I sat there staring at the clipping. When I had first learned of Eric's homosexuality, I had heard the echo within my memory of a boy saying as he went to bed, "Tell Dad to come in when he comes home." I had felt the hunger of a boy for love from a man, his father, and when that hunger had not been satisfied, it had turned into a different kind of hunger for love from a man.

But I had had only a hunch, an intuition. Here was a psychiatrist, trained and knowledgeable, who had made huge samplings. He was not a woman deserted by her husband.

I went downtown to the Minneapolis Public Library and got Dr. Bieber's book. It was not a book one would expect to curl up with and read avidly on a long winter evening. Nevertheless I did, though I skipped most of the statistical analysis. It was the case histories that interested me.

I began to understand a few of the implications contained in Dr. Bieber's apparently simple and unequivocal statement, "I have concluded that given a good father-son relationship no boy develops a homosexual pattern."[2] One implication seemed to be that a man who had difficulty relating to his son might also have difficulty relating to others, including his wife, if I could judge from the case histories. In fact, a father with problems often seemed to presuppose a mother with problems.

I thought back over the years to a time when I had spent three weeks at a Christian rehabilitation center because I was at the end of my rope. I happened to be there over Mother's Day, and some well-intentioned woman came to give a little talk appropriate to the season. She dwelt on clichés of how our mothers loved us more than anyone else in the whole world, our mothers understood us best, our mothers had done the best for us, and on and on.

As she talked the group became increasingly rude and disruptive. We knew that we were behaving childishly, but we seemed unable to stop ourselves. Afterward, when we compared notes, we discovered that more than half the group were there because of severe mother problems.

The director of the center pointed out to us that while the domineering mother was most visible and received the most hostility and blame, she could not have played out her role without the acquiescence of a passive husband.

"You think it is only a mother problem," he said. "Make no mistake about it. It is also very much a father problem. It doesn't seem so at first glance only because the mother is dominant and the father is passive."

As I read Bieber's book, there were many times when I cringed. For example, I apparently would qualify, at least to some extent, as a "CBI mother." The initials stood for close-binding-intimate. God knows I had not set out to be a CBI mother. I would have said it was the last kind of mother I wanted to be. Somehow circumstances had betrayed me.

Not that either Tom or I had perpetrated the excesses detailed in Bieber's book. I had neither bathed Eric when he was eleven years old, as had one mother (I think that Eric banished me from the bathroom when he was four or five), nor had I allowed him to crawl into bed with me, nor had he been made to sleep in a room with his sisters. I had not undressed in front of him. Tom's and my lovemaking had not been flaunted before the children; it had taken place behind closed doors.[3]

Still, there were a number of faint echoes of our family life here and there in Bieber's book. Tom had not made Eric a homosexual, nor had I—alone. It had been like two muddy streams flowing together. There was no possible way these two could join forces and produce a sparkling clear river.

Some time before, I had had a strange and rather horrible dream. A wedding was taking place, but the bridegroom was headless. The bride finally appeared, a radiant vision in white, jewel-encrusted satin, but veiled. At last, just before the ceremony was to be performed, someone in horror finally plucked up courage to point out to the bride that she was marrying a headless man. In answer, the bride lifted her veil to show a horribly disfigured face. "Who else would have me?" she said. "He'll never know."

The wounded masculine married to the disfigured feminine—how often was that drama replayed, with infinite variations, in actual life? And what of the children of these unions? Their perceptions of what makes a whole, psychologically healthy man or woman were damaged from the moment of birth. They had no models of wholeness, no healthy integration of masculine and feminine elements in either father or mother.

I had only recently been introduced through my work with Lee to the idea of "masculine and feminine elements." Dr. Carl G. Jung, she had told me, had developed a two-pronged concept which he termed the *anima* and the *animus*. It was the idea that every man also has within him some feminine elements or an unconscious feminine "side," which Jung termed the *anima*, the feminine form of the Latin word for *soul*. Inside every woman were unconscious masculine elements, which Dr. Jung called by the masculine form of the word, *animus*.[4]

In our marriage Tom and I had supposed there were two people, Tom and Mary. In reality there were four aspects present, at the most simplified: Tom's masculine side and his *anima*, my feminine side and my *animus*. The destructive part was that too often the negative side of his *anima* had brought out the negative side of my *animus*, and vice versa.

There had been many times as our marriage deteriorated when I had seen that we brought out the worst in each other rather than the best. We had reinforced each other downward rather than upward. But though we could see what was happening and longed to do it differently, we never seemed to be able to find out how to get from a downward spiral to an upward one. Even the counselors we had seen had been unable to help us do this.

So both Tom and I had contributed to Eric's homosexual orientation because neither of us had been whole. Neither of us had had a good integration of our masculine and feminine elements.

As I thought about these matters I began to see that this line of reasoning created some theological problems. If it was true that Tom's and my psychological problems had predisposed Eric toward homosexuality, how much free will had he been able to exercise? Had he made his choice of the homosexual way of life as a free agent? Had he chosen a "sinful" way because he willfully wanted to sin? Or had he been pushed, by inner compulsions that he hardly grasped, into this "sinful" orientation? If, as he had told me, he had had inklings of homosexual leanings when he was five, this hardly seemed like a rational choice.

What then of Paul's vehement denunciations of homosexuality, which could be summed up in the words, "Do not be deceived; . . . homosexuals . . . will [not] inherit the kingdom of God."[5]

If a person is a physical cripple because of malformation of the body, it is not a sin. What about the psychological malformation of a person, an emotional crippling for which the person is not responsible? Is this a sin when physical crippling is not? Neither person is responsible for his or her condition. It has been given to the individual at birth, by heredity and environment.

Where is God in all this? If a person is condemned because of his or her hereditary personality responding to the conditioning of the environment into which that person has been born, is this not the most devastating kind of predestination?

There had to be, I decided, some missing factors in the theology of homosexuality to which I had subscribed. It was not quite so simple as the Community of the Resurrection—and many other churches and denominations—had supposed.

If Tom and I were responsible for Eric's "sinful" orientation, would he suffer eternal damnation or would we? But our orientation came out of the patterns in our homes. So, in a way, we were no more responsible for our problems than Eric was for his. We were all, as Dr. Theodore Isaac Rubin has said, "victims of victims."[6]

One thing seemed immediately and abundantly clear to me: there were no neat, pat answers such as I had been led to believe. The situation was far more complex than I had imagined. Maybe I ought to begin seeking some more credible answers.

Because I wanted to know what evangelical writers had to say about homosexuality, I went to an evangelical bookstore in Minneapolis. I summoned up my courage and asked in a normal tone of voice, looking the clerk straight in the eye, "What books do you have dealing with homosexuality?"

The clerk was equal to the occasion. Her expression remained carefully neutral. Her voice betrayed nothing as she said, "I think we have a book on that subject." *A* book, I thought. It was a large store.

She searched and searched. "We had one on that subject," she said finally, "but I can't seem to find it."

I left my name and telephone number in case she located it.

Next day I received a call that she had found the elusive volume. I was faintly amused—I thought it unlikely that they would so mislay a book on, for example, evangelism.

I was a little disappointed in the book, *What About Homosexuality?* by Clinton R. Jones. It was written dispassionately and contained the usual statements of those who do not see homosexuality as a sin but as one orientation of several. It held out less hope of cure than of helping the person not to feel guilty about his or her sexual orientation.

There was food for thought, however, in some of the statements. The homosexual, for example, must be willing and able to commit a good many hours and dollars to counseling if a change is to be brought about.[7]

I recalled a more detailed statement about this which I had read in Dr. Bieber's book:

> Of the forty patients whose analyses were of 150 to 349 hours duration, nine (23 percent) became heterosexual. Of the group who had 350 or more therapeutic sessions, eighteen (47 percent) achieved the shift to heterosexuality. . . . Clearly, the homosexual who remains in treatment above 150 hours is much more likely to achieve a heterosexual adaptation.[8]

Was the kingdom of heaven therefore closed to homosexuals if they did not have the requisite time and money? Somehow that didn't seem like sound theology to me.

Another question in Jones's book that struck me was, where are we to find enough qualified therapists to help all the homosexuals?[9] Where, indeed! Is one therefore lost because there is no therapist available? That didn't seem like sound theology either.

And what is considered a cure? Simply ceasing to be a practicing homosexual but with unchanged sexual orientation? Through close friends I had heard of several of these persons, and I had to acknowledge that the picture they gave me was bleak. "A very lonely life," one friend said. "He keeps himself very busy."

"He's tried to commit suicide several times lately," another friend said to me of the Christian homosexual she knew.

Somehow something was missing in these "cures." Jesus had promised "life in all its fullness."[10] If it was to be a real cure, then the cured one should be able to enter with joy and real fulfillment into heterosexual life, able to marry and beget children with no emotional reservations.

It was all very confusing.

One thing I was sure of: there didn't seem to be any easy answers to the problem of homosexuality and the Christian life. At one time I had thought there were. Now I was beginning to see that there were no easy answers at all.

12

Rocks

Some years before, when I was immersed in Agnes Sanford's books, I went to communion one Sunday morning determined to do something for a woman named Eleanor. She was a widow, a member of the congregation, a rather unsophisticated, uneducated woman who had had a sad and damaging childhood.

I cannot remember now in what way I thought I was going to "help" Eleanor. Apologies are due to Mrs. Sanford for my total misunderstanding of what she meant when she wrote of saying prayers of "special intention" in a communion service for someone on her prayer list.[1] At no time, in any of her books, did she ever advocate doing what I tried to do that day.

To myself I pictured the depths of Eleanor's unconscious as a deep ocean with dark stones at the bottom. These stones represented resentment, anger, and the like at those who had wounded her. During the communion service I pictured myself with a crowbar prying those stones off the bottom of the ocean. God forgive me!

After the service as we were leaving the church, Eleanor spoke to me. "I had the oddest experience in church this morning," she said with some agitation. "As I was sitting there in communion, it was just as if a huge load of dirt fell down in front of me."

I can tell you, I was scared! It was the first and the last time I ever attempted anything like it. Evidently I had made some kind of connection with Eleanor, but what kind? I felt I had wandered into a psychic mine field. Fortunately, little damage seemed to have been done, but I was not going to explore in such dangerous territory again.

Had the load of dirt been Eleanor's or mine?

For that matter, whose rocks had I been prying up, hers or mine? Because I imagined that there were also rocks deep in the ocean of my unconscious, perhaps they were mine.

If one of those rocks could be raised, would it have shattered when it got to the surface? Would it have spread all kinds of hideous, tarry debris upon the surface of the water? I rather imagined that it would.

Where do such images come from? How do they spring into consciousness? What made me visualize my unconscious as an ocean? What made me suppose that there were rocks on the floor of my unconscious? What made me think the rocks would explode when brought to the surface?

Some years earlier, when I had been at the Christian rehabilitation center, my counselor had talked to me about confession. Was it a part of my prayer life? he had asked.

To this day my answer astounds me. I told him that I never felt able to confess very much because somehow it seemed to me that if I allowed even a little guilt to come, so much more would follow that I would surely be swept away by it.

How did I know? How could I have guessed? What intuition told me?

For almost a year now Lee and I had been excavating in my unconscious, slowly and gently picking away at one tight, hard layer after another.

Early in life, when I was one or two or three, it must somehow have been conveyed to me that anger was bad. From then on, without my knowing it, a continual metamorphosis had been going on inside me. The living vegetation of anger had been stifled, pushed down into the primeval swamp of the unconscious, and maintained there under tons of pressure until at last it was as dense, as hard as coal.

Anger. Wrath. Hatred. Rage.

"Let not the sun go down upon your wrath."[2] Of course. It will cool, it will solidify, and it will lie there at the bottom of the ocean of the unconscious like hunks of hardened lava. It will not go away.

Roget's Thesaurus, with its objective listing of words, begins by listing synonyms for wrath as resentment, displeasure, vexation, irritation. Soon the list progresses to bitter resentment, bitterness of spirit, virulence, vindictiveness, hate.[3] Dispassionately it is reflecting the process by which the molten lava of anger hardens in the unconscious into the granite of unremitting rage.

"You have heard that it was said to the men of old, 'You shall not kill; and whoever kills shall be liable to judgment,' " Jesus said. "But I say to you that every one who is angry with his brother shall be liable to judgment."[4]

And because I was subtly programmed from birth onward to be a "good little girl," I denied anger. If one was in danger of judgment because one was angry, I would insure myself against judgment by not being angry.

I had no idea that it was impossible to do this. I didn't even know I was trying to do it.

Undoubtedly Lee had perceived the outlines of solidified anger early in our working together. But I had not been in touch enough with my real feelings or my real self for her to be able to say anything.

At last—*at last*—a dream surfaced that pointed the way. In my dream, against a dark background, I saw a tree that had corrosive fruit. A few of the fruits were brown, but a few were a hard, bright-green color, like small stylized apples such as are used on topiary trees. I threw some of these apples into a bonfire, and the smoke from the fire created sore spots on my legs and ate holes in my nylons.

Lee and I talked about this dream, and I tried to bring up

associations that it awakened. I called it "The Corrosive Tree" because the burning fruit made smoke that ate away flesh and fabric.

"Could you name some corrosive things?" Lee asked me.

Acids, lye, rust—none of these physical agents even occurred to me.

"Fear is," I answered thoughtfully. "And anger. Anger is very, very corrosive."

"Is it anger that is eating at your legs and your stockings?" she asked.

I looked at her for a long time. "Yes," I said at last. "It could very well be anger."

The dream of the tree had opened a path into the almost inexhaustible storehouse of hoarded wrath within me. Lee suggested that I might be interested in reading *The Angry Book* by Dr. Theodore Isaac Rubin. He talked about a "slush fund of perverted emotions,"[5] his principal concern in the book being the slush fund of unacknowledged, unexpressed anger. When he spoke of a "slush fund hemorrhage"[6] or a "slush fund explosion"[7] I could remember a few of these in my lifetime, when what had happened to trigger the explosion was small and the reaction was out of proportion to the provocation.

"But what do I do with anger?" I asked Lee.

"You feel it," she answered. "You express it."

"But how?" I wanted to know. One of the prime targets of my anger was dead. Even if the target were alive, you could hardly go around shouting at and punching the person.

"Write out your anger," she suggested.

I did. I began on normal-size pieces of paper with neat writing, but as time went on I felt a need for a larger area. At length I was printing violent messages on huge sheets of newsprint with thick red and black crayons. (Thin ones broke under the pressure.) The words I used were not nice or polite at all. Good little girls *never* used words like that.

But there was Lee, commending me for each angry explosion with which I presented her.

I found that words were often not enough. Sometimes I pounded my pillow or my mattress while I told someone (in my imagination) what I really thought of him or her. Often tears would stream down my face. Sometimes I would punch an imaginary punching bag or kick my imaginary adversary. I bought plasticene clay, and sometimes I would slam a wad of clay against my clipboard over and over and over. I even drew a particular face on the clipboard and pounded that face with the clay again and again.

How could it be good to express anger? All my life I had been led to think that it was bad. Yet now, when I allowed myself to *feel* anger, even old anger stored away years before, I had to acknowledge that good things were happening to me. After a session of feeling and expressing anger, I would suddenly be filled with energy and accomplish a great deal. Or I could fall asleep easily that night and sleep an unbroken eight hours, something I had hardly been able to do for forty years. Or I would suddenly find tension within my body lessened. Feeling and expressing anger couldn't be all bad.

A verse from John popped into my head: "You will know the truth, and the truth will make you free."[8]

But anger was a sin. What I had been pouring out on paper, what I had been expressing by beating the mattress and the air and my clipboard, was not pretty. It was actually very ugly.

And suddenly it all jelled. As long as I had kept the anger hidden, it could not be confessed. Jesus could not help me with a sin of which I was unaware. He knew about it, but until I allowed it to emerge from its hiding place, I prevented him from touching that sin. The salvation which Jesus offered, which he had bought at such a terrible price, was going unused until the sin was faced and brought to Jesus through confession.

The idea was not to try to be so good that one didn't need salvation. If one was real and honest, one began to see that it was humanly impossible to be that good. The key, rather, was to face up to what one really was, the sins one had committed, and to confess them before God and to ask forgiveness.

As I allowed more and more of the repressed anger to emerge, I began to understand what John meant when he wrote, "Any one who hates his brother is a murderer."[9] It was true. There were times when I pounded the mattress that the idea of hitting my victim again and again with a knife occurred to me. Just for a second I could have murdered because of that anger.

And I would remember the days in the past when, if I thought of suicide, I would think of slashing my wrists with a butcher knife. Mentally it had always seemed to me that if one really wanted to kill oneself, carbon monoxide in a closed garage was the efficient, painless way. Strangely, this method had never tempted me in the least. The thought of a butcher knife had.

I began to understand the whole web that had entrapped me. Repressed anger continued to gather interest until it found release somehow.

There was only one way out. That way was not to deaden anger and deny it. Nor was it to release the anger by violence against another or against oneself. The real escape was to feel, to acknowledge—and to confess.

"O God," I cried, throwing myself on my bed, weeping, "I have sinned. Over and over and over. I have been angry. I have hated. I understand why you have linked anger to murder. I know that deep down inside me there is a hidden murderer. I confess it all. Forgive me."

As I lay there I became aware of several things. "Good Mary" was dead. In fact, maybe "good Mary" had never existed. Maybe she had been simply a creation of my imagination. There was, in reality, only "bad Mary," who hated and got angry. Or maybe there was only real Mary, human Mary. There would never be any other Mary. I had been fooling myself all along.

I would never be good. I would always be made of clay, some of it very ugly clay.

But there was help. It could be expressed only in symbolism, in imagery. The robe of *his* righteousness (not mine) to cover my faulty clay. His blood shed instead of mine. Washed in his blood (a gruesome thought if taken literally, but glorious beyond imagining if taken as a symbolic expression of God's love for me). The Lamb sacrificed to make atonement for *me*. "This is my body, which is broken for *you*."[10] "I have come in order that *you* may have life."[11] He had bought that life at the price of his own body.

Who could understand it? Who could explain it? Who could mentally make sense of it?

It was something that could only be experienced. "For now we see in a mirror dimly, but then face to face. Now I know in part; then I shall understand fully, even as I have been fully understood."[12] I had always supposed that in this verse Paul was talking about how it would be in heaven. And so he probably was.

But now, in the moment of confession, I felt a foretaste of that heaven. Because I now understood myself much more fully, I no longer had to strain, to strive, to force upon myself an impossible, painful mask of "goodness." All along I had been fooling only myself with that mask; all along *I had been fully understood.* God had seen the smoldering fires within, and with gentle fingers through Lee had lifted layer upon layer upon layer, until at last the burning hell within me had been laid bare.

That is how it must have been when Jesus was alive, I thought. He had looked at a sinner, had merely said, "Your sins are forgiven," and the person was changed.

Evidently a transaction had taken place which the Gospel writers were unable to imprison on paper. The eyes of Jesus had looked through the outer layers of self-deception deep into the central being of the person. Suddenly the person must have seen him or her self as he or she really was.

And in that moment of the death of the false self there was a tremendous release—and relief. There was no longer need to spend energy pretending. One was known as one was, but—this was the completely unexpected and healing reality—one was not rejected. One was loved with a white-hot intensity that seemed to burn up the sin and cleanse and refine. Love. What a burning and shining thing divine love is, I realized. Not the namby-pamby sentimental mush I had supposed.

At the moment when I had finally seen the real me—the ugliness of the real Mary—at the moment of the death of "good Mary," at the moment of dropping the mask, life had begun to come out of death.

13

"My Wounded Ones"

It began as an ordinary Sunday morning service at the Community of the Resurrection. A large number of the church's young people had been feeling for some time that they were called into various kinds of mission service and had been talking to Paul Sundstrom and the elders about it. This particular Sunday morning Paul preached a sermon entitled "Going Out to Meet the Needs of Others."

When he had finished there was a prophecy, whether through Paul or someone else I do not remember. The burden of the prophecy ran thus: "I am calling you to service from all spectrums of age and maturity. Do not compare yourself to others. Let my Spirit reveal to you the place I would have you go."

Following that, Paul asked us to turn in our hymnals to "Just as I Am." I had sung this hymn hundreds of times, and I had never particularly liked it. That day the words suddenly came alive to me: "Just as I am, without one plea/But that thy blood was shed for me,/And that thou bid'st me come to thee . . ."[1] And I saw, as I had never seen before, that the hymn was talking about me. Before, it had always been referring to sinners—other people—but not to me because mostly I was a "good" girl.

Tears ran down my cheeks as we came to the words "Just as I am, and waiting not/To rid my soul of one dark blot." There were so many dark blots, so much hardened lava of ancient anger and rage and hatred within me.

"Just as I am, thou wilt receive,/Wilt welcome, pardon, cleanse, relieve." I knew what the hymn was talking about. Firsthand, I knew.

"Just as I am, thy love unknown/Has broken every barrier down." When I had faced my inner ugliness, I had felt that love as I had never felt it before, real and actual. In spite of that ugliness I knew he loved me.

There remained only the need for my response. It was not a new response, for I had given it years before, but it came now with a new intensity. "Now, to be thine, yea, thine alone,/O Lamb of God, I come—I come!" I felt like a broken child running home to her father—"Daddy, I'm coming, I'm coming!"—and flinging herself into those outstretched arms.

And as we sang and tears ran down my cheeks and I realized that Jesus had reached out to me not because I was already good but because I needed him so desperately, the Lord suddenly dropped a message into my mind: "That's how homosexuals are to come to me."

No difference between the homosexual and me. Straight or gay, we were both sinners. Was homosexuality a greater sin than anger? Or, I suddenly realized, than spiritual pride? On a scale of one to twenty, where would the various sins fall? Perhaps there was no scale, because all had sinned; there was only One without sin.

As we finished singing "Just as I Am" it seemed as if the Lord was saying to me, "Have I not called even these my children, my wounded ones? All you have to do is tell them of my love. I will do the rest."

There was no need for me to ask who "my wounded ones" were. I was very much aware that God had not said, "my sinful ones," but "my wounded ones." God had said nothing about sin at all. "All you have to do is tell them of my love."

Suddenly I remembered how Jesus had dealt with the Pharisees who brought him the woman taken in adultery. He had said, "Let him who is without sin among you be the first to throw a stone at her."[2] Could a murderer cast a stone at a homosexual? Who was so pure that he or she could mete out judgment to another?

The Lord had never intended that human beings should judge others. That was God's prerogative. The human task was to tell others of God's love. Only moments before, God had instructed me to "tell them that I love them."

How could God love them? They were not good.

But neither was I good.

What I had said and what I had thought were really two different theologies. I had *said*, "God so loved the *world*...."[3] Not the good people. The world. But I saw now that I had really thought God loved only those who belonged to the church and who tried to be "good." I had fallen into the same trap as had the Pharisees.

Jesus had said to the Pharisees, "Those who are well have no need of a physician, but those who are sick. . . . For I came not to call the righteous, but sinners."[4] And again, "The tax collectors and the harlots go into the kingdom of God before you."[5] Because those outside the pale knew their need, but the Pharisees felt they had no need.

The standard for coming to Christ was not goodness. It was need.

"My wounded ones." (Not "sinners.") "Tell them that I love them." And then that sentence that removed all responsibility for judgment from me, that made me feel that these words really were from God: "I will do the rest."

14

From Judgment
to Love

To have a flash of intuition or insight is one thing. To begin to live by that new insight is quite another.

In the days that followed I felt as if a tornado had suddenly demolished my secure house. Figuratively I was left standing, shivering and fearful, on a hill that had been stripped of all familiar vegetation and structures. The unconscious premises and suppositions on which I had built my half-century of life were gone. I could understand, I thought, how a turtle might feel if it were suddenly yanked from its protective shell and left naked.

Outwardly my life flowed on in its usual channels. I went to work certain days of the week, kept my appointments with Lee, performed the necessary household chores. June came. Barbara was graduated from high school, and soon she settled into her summer job.

Inwardly I was on a quest. Day after day the question confronted me, if being a Christian doesn't mean being good, what does it mean?

If I was to be honest with myself, I had to admit that my definition of being a Christian went something like this: believing that Jesus is the Son of God and that he died for my sins; being a church member; being active in church programs; not drinking or smoking; staying out of bars; not gambling; not "sleeping around"; not swearing; not being angry; loving everyone; being kind.

I realized there were a good many nots on my list. There didn't seem to be much positive thrust in my definition of being a Christian.

One night as I was reading the Bible, I came upon the calling of Matthew. It was only one verse. "As Jesus passed on from there, he saw a man called Matthew sitting at the tax office; and he said to him, 'Follow me.' And he rose and followed him."[1] Only two words, and Matthew's whole way of life was changed. "He left everything," Luke adds in his version of the story.[2]

As I pondered this brief account, I began to understand what being a Christian really means.

Here was a man who had sacrificed something very precious according to Jewish standards in order to acquire wealth. He had been willing to become an outcast from Jewish society so that he might satisfy his love for money and possessions. And now a dusty itinerant preacher walked by, looked at him, and said, "Follow me." The tax collector stood up, left behind him the world he had chosen at such great cost, and walked off after Jesus. Why?

Was there something in the way Jesus looked at Matthew, something the Gospel writer could not put into words, which captured Matthew and took him away forever from the old life of greed and extortion?

I noticed that Jesus never said a word about Matthew's business, for or against. He simply issued an invitation. Apparently the invitation was to something so interesting or attractive or compelling that Matthew left everything—all that he had lived for before—and followed. What was that compelling force?

Jesus laid out no ground rules. He gave no doctrine. He did

not discuss anything with Matthew. All he said was, "Follow me."

Follow *me*. Not a system. Not rules or laws. Matthew was not subscribing with his head to a philosophy or a religion. He was following a person.

Long ago he had traded a religious system for things, possessions. Now he was trading possessions for something greater. What was Jesus offering him that was so compelling? It was—it had to be—love. In the person of Jesus, love had walked down to where Matthew was and had held out his hand.

Now a new thought occurred to me. Why in the world had Jesus invited Matthew? It certainly wasn't because Matthew was so holy. Nor was it in order to curry favor with the establishment. In fact, calling Matthew to be a disciple carried an absolute guarantee of alienating the establishment. Why had Jesus done it?

In a flash of understanding I saw that Jesus did not call people because they were good. If that had been the case, he would have surrounded himself with scribes and Pharisees. He called those who had needs. When he called, he was offering something.

Suddenly I saw this whole process in relation to myself. Jesus had called me, years before, not because I was so good but because I was so broken. I had not known it at the time. I had felt, I now realized, that Jesus was simply putting his seal of approval on the good little girl I thought I was. In reality he had known how shattered I was, had waited patiently for me to invite him in, and had begun reconstruction as soon as he had firmly established my trust in him.

All my life, while mouthing the correct words that "God is love," I had really believed unconsciously that God is judgment. From my earliest years onward, I had been exposed much more to judgment than to acceptance. Always my ideas were judged and found wanting. I never measured up. First with my mother and later with Tom I was always wrong. My ideas—and therefore my self—were worthless.

Not until I had come into contact with Lee had I begun to

experience real acceptance. It was difficult to define exactly how she had demonstrated acceptance and therefore love. Partly it was because she listened and heard what I was saying and could reflect it back to me accurately. She was not listening only in order to contradict me. She was not passing judgment on what I was saying. She treated my words and my thoughts as if they had value. They might be quite erroneous, but somehow they had a value and deserved consideration because . . . because I had value.

Simply because I was a person made in the image of God, I had value. In our sessions together week after week Lee had been God's intermediary, reflecting to me God's evaluation of myself: "You are of great worth to me. Not because you are right. Sometimes you are very wrong. That has nothing to do with it. You are of great value to me simply because you *are*."

Jesus' communication to Matthew, stripped to the bare essentials, must have been something like, "I *care*, because you *are*." Suddenly Matthew no longer needed possessions in order to give himself worth. Simply because he was Matthew he mattered. Of course he was willing to part with things. He needed something far more. He needed a relationship with a person who had made him feel like a person of worth.

Not *a worthy person*. That seemed to carry overtones of judgment, of rightness or wrongness.

A person of worth carried no such judgment. It was a statement of the essential value of a human being. Any human being. On God's scale the worst criminal weighed as much as the greatest king, the greatest saint.

No system of thought, no book of rules, no theology was adequate to convey this to a person. Only a relationship could do it. A relationship to Jesus. To the Christ.

If this was so, I reasoned, then this relationship with Christ must have some of the characteristics of a relationship with any ordinary person. The relationship would not remain static; after the initial contact it would either grow or decrease. In order for it to grow, one would have to have frequent contacts. Contact as part of a large group could never substitute for a one-to-one contact; it could only augment the face-to-face relationship.

Neither could talking about the relationship, defining it, or drawing up rules to govern it substitute for the relationship itself. Talking about marriage, for example, or laying down guidelines for it was totally different from actually being married.

Being a Christian, I finally saw, was being loved by God—and loving in return.

And now a question occurred to me that had never before entered my mind. Had Matthew's sacrifice of all he wanted in life been worth it? Had he gained something he would not have had if he had remained a tax collector?

The Bible was silent about this. I could only look within my own life and guess that perhaps what was true for me was true for Matthew also. I thought of the uncounted times that I had felt the response of God to me when I had asked a question, when I had felt some pressure from the Spirit on my spirit, when at a crucial moment God had in some way spoken to my need.

How does one describe the indescribable? How can one explain the piercing sweetness of knowing God has heard one's cry, has answered one's (stupid) question, has not said, "That's too trivial. Go away. Don't bother me." Of course Matthew's sacrifice had been worth it. He had found a fullness of life he had never received from his possessions.

As I looked back on my own experiences I saw something else. Whenever I came to Jesus Christ with a question, a request, a cry for help, he had never said, "I'm sorry, I can't help until you become good." He had seen that great mass of rocks in my unconscious. They were not hidden from him. But he had never turned away from me because of them. He had never withheld himself or cut off our relationship until I became good.

In no way, I saw, had God given me what I deserved. I should have received judgment. Instead, I had received nothing but love.

15

Butchina

"Every dream has a meaning," Lee had once said to me.

I had looked at her unbelievingly. "*Every* dream?" I had asked.

She had looked at me unflinchingly. "*Every* dream," she had repeated.

I thought of some of the strange, unpleasant dreams I had had. Some were so embarrassing I hesitated telling them even to Lee. Others seemed merely a rehash of recent events, thoroughly mixed and garbled, often ridiculous or impossible.

"Every dream is telling us something," she had said. "Most often it is something about the forgotten parts of ourselves. We may not be able to interpret every dream immediately," she had added, "because we may not have enough data. Even a fragment of a dream may have an important message."

One midsummer night I had a dream. On waking, I could remember only one thing from the dream, a vivid image of an incredibly ugly little figure hurrying to get through a set of double doors which were closing or which, perhaps, had just been thrown open.

I sat down and painted the figure, a short, squat woman incongruously dressed in a ruffled, ice-blue satin pannier, with an ice-blue satin mobcap on her black unkempt hair.

Surprisingly, I felt that for once I had drawn exactly what I had set out to draw. The figure before me on paper was the figure I had seen in my dream. I had even managed to capture the feeling that the little figure was hurrying.

"Look," I said when I showed the drawing to Lee, "this is the first time I have drawn a figure that looks free and uninhibited." I pulled out some of my earlier drawings. The women in these drawings were "prettier"—neater, smoother—but somehow much more constricted. They were tidy, conforming shells. The ugly one had life, a raw vitality, a vigor that the carefully pretty, restricted ones did not have.

After some minutes of contemplating the drawing, Lee asked, "What is her name?"

I began to ponder. What would be the name of such a grotesque person?

"Don't think," she said. "Just give me a name off the top of your head."

I snapped off a name and immediately felt cold prickles run down my spine. I looked at Lee, and she looked at me.

No one would ever christen a child with such a name. From what recess of my mind had it emerged? The name I had given was Butchina. I began to be aware that the drawing I had made might have far-reaching consequences.

"Why don't you go home and have a dialogue with her?" Lee gestured toward the drawing. "What would she say to you? What would you say to her? Spend some time with her. Get to know her—who she is, where she came from."

I went home, sat down, and wrote out an imaginary dialogue with Butchina. It was not a difficult assignment. Butchina seemed only too ready to talk, and most of it was rather earthy. I almost blushed as I wrote.

I began to understand what C. G. Jung meant when he wrote that "the images have a life of their own and that the symbolic events develop according to their own logic."[1]

If I had been able to, I would have sent Butchina back where she had come from. By now, however, I had learned enough from Lee to know that this was not possible or desirable. Butchina would only kick up far more trouble in my unconscious than she could out in the open where I could keep my eye on her.

At my next appointment Lee and I discussed the imaginary dialogue with Butchina.

"Butchina is appalling," I said. "I wish I could send her away."

Lee said gently, "She belongs to you. She's part of you. Can you give her a place in your life?"

"Ugh," I said. "I don't want to."

"She doesn't have to take over and do whatever she wants," Lee said. "You're still in control. You can set the boundaries. But she does need some space."

We sat for a few minutes looking at the painting of Butchina.

"Why do you find her appalling?" Lee asked finally.

"Well," I said slowly, trying to sort out my feelings of revulsion, "she's so . . . grotesque."

Lee was silent, waiting.

"She's a grown woman, but she's like a midget—much too short. She's never grown up. By her clothing she's saying she's a woman. But she's abnormal. She's both a man and a woman." I had discovered this through the dialogue with Butchina. "And it wouldn't make any difference whether she dressed as a man or a woman, her face would be just as ugly either way."

There was a silence. I kept hearing myself saying, "She's never grown up."

And I kept remembering how my sister, Meg, and I had known for a long time that in some ways Mother had never outgrown the effects of her father's death when she was five years old. Psychologically it had stunted her as surely as if she had been kept all her life in a very small straitjacket. Emotionally she had never grown up.

Butchina. A grotesque mixture of masculine and feminine. Ugly either way. Was that how I had seen my mother? If I was going to be brutally honest with myself, the answer was yes. I shrank from such honesty because the painful frightening question which followed was, how much was I like my mother?

I had to voice the awful thought. "Is that me?" I asked Lee, pointing to the painting of Butchina.

She regarded me soberly. "I don't know," she said. "Is it?"

I stared hard at the little figure.

"Ask her," Lee suggested.

Tears gathered in my eyes. "I'm afraid."

"It might be worse not to know," she said quietly. "Worse to keep wondering."

"I'll ask her this week," I said. I'd had all I could take at the moment.

But I kept putting if off. As long as I didn't know, I at least had hope. I would have a conversation with Butchina tomorrow. Or the next day. Or the next.

One night I dreamed I was standing before a very small doorway. Somehow I knew that I was being commanded to unlock the door and work my way through it to the other side. I had no idea what I would find beyond the door. I knew only that I was being ordered, that there was no possibility of refusal.

I awoke in a cold sweat, my heart pounding. What was the door I was supposed to unlock? But, of course, I knew. I had a question I must ask Butchina. Sleep would be impossible until I had done it.

Turning on the lamp by my bed, I hunted up the painting of Butchina. I looked at her a long time in revulsion and loathing. At last I said aloud, "Butchina, are you me?"

There was a long silence. Finally in the stillness I remembered my voice saying long before to Lee, "I almost think I could diagram why Eric is homosexual."

"I think I'll see if I *can* diagram it," I thought now. I reached for paper and began. Almost at once I realized this was far too big a task for four o'clock in the morning.

Several days passed before I completed the diagram, inked and painted it. The results were astounding. Previously I had known all the facts that were assembled on the diagram. There was no new information. But as I arranged the information in family-tree form, noting the characteristics and life situations of my parents and their parents as well as of Tom's side of the family, I could see a pattern emerging. There was not a single strong male figure anywhere. In one way or another, sweetly, genteelly, or horribly, the women dominated.

I thought of Helen M. Luke's description of Éowyn, niece-daughter of Theoden, King of the Mark, in Tolkien's *The Return of the King:* "Born into a family in which, perhaps, the father has succumbed to the softness of his anima while the mother, as mother, is simply absent, since she is buried in a mass of animus opinions, the daughter is brought up without a clear image of either masculine or feminine."[2]

All down the line there had been psychic wounding and shaping of the masculine and feminine sides of Tom's and my forebears. Those wounds had been passed down the line as if they had been fed into a giant funnel until at last they had been channeled through Tom and me and had come to full fruition in Eric. He was no freak of nature, no strange, unrelated accident. He was the logical outcome of his psychic inheritance.

I turned the diagram over and wrote the title for it on the back: "We Have Met the Enemy and He Is *Us.*" Pogo's words had never been truer.

16

Troy
Perry

One day I was in the library looking for a book on homosexuality that Eric had suggested I read. As my eyes scanned the
shelves, a title suddenly leaped out at me, *The Lord Is My
Shepherd and He Knows I'm Gay.*

I stood rooted to the spot for what seemed like minutes. Half
of me, in righteous wrath, wanted to call down fire from heaven
and zap the blasphemous book right off the shelf. The other half
of me was saying, "But that's just what you've been saying the
Lord was saying to you."

At last, with the same reluctance I would have felt picking up
a snake, I put out my hand and plucked the book off the shelf.
I took it home.

I could have read many books that would have educated my
mind about the gay world. This one kicked me in the solar
plexus. Reading it was an experience that challenged me on
every front.

The book is written by the Rev. Troy Perry, founder and at
that time pastor of the Metropolitan Community Church, the

first gay church and denomination. It is the story of his life and struggles up to the point when the book was written.

As I read, I was angry; I was frightened; I was appalled; I wept; I laughed; I cheered. Whether I agreed with what he was saying or not, I was totally involved!

Though I had talked a little with Eric and Brian about the problems of social and economic justice for the homosexual, they had come into the struggle for civil rights comparatively recently. They had therefore never borne the full brunt of discrimination against gays. Besides that, Minneapolis is one of the better places for gays to live. I had not been aware of what it was like to be a member of a despised and outcast minority. I wept as I read. *I had not known.*

In Perry's book gays are real people, not outlandish freaks, depersonalized statistics, or sinners of a deeper dye than all others. They are people who hurt just like other people— perhaps more so, because life for them is often more of an uphill battle.

There was the young man, a homosexual, who came to Los Angeles from San Francisco and went to a gay bar. He ended up being arrested in the bar, supposedly for solicitation. The next morning they "picked his body out of a lake." He had been a teacher in San Francisco. His family and his school board knew nothing of his sexual orientation, and he could not face their finding out.[1]

Another young man who was planning to commit suicide phoned Perry in the middle of the night. Perry and another man from the church drove over and talked to him.

> He found that someone cared. We helped him. And he's been an active member ever since.
>
> That started our Crisis Intervention Committee. Volunteers came forward to man the phone around the clock. Others stood by to go out and see what they could do to help. We began to get training from professionals who could help us in suicide prevention, and in counseling for acceptance.[2]

103

I felt stricken as I read this. I had not realized that gays had problems with the most fundamental concerns of human life: problems with jobs and housing, and consequently with providing themselves with the necessities of life. The Metropolitan Community Church dealt with those areas of life where public welfare and heterosexual Christian churches had failed, had turned their backs, or had been utterly ignorant of the problem.

There were other stories that made me cringe.

"Did you weep," wrote Perry in a circular he mailed to heterosexual churches, "when [a homosexual] was beaten to death by the police in Los Angeles? When another was shot in the back and killed in a park in Berkeley? And another imprisoned for life in Florida?"[3]

Imprisoned for life? Was this the twentieth century he was writing about or an eighteenth-century New England witch-hunt? I was appalled.

Before reading Perry's book I had naively assumed that the protection of the law was the same for everyone. How could I have been so simpleminded, so Pollyannaish?

Perry was put in jail one night during a sit-in to bring about changes in repressive and discriminatory laws against homosexuals. "Then I heard a ruckus start in some other cell," he wrote. "I heard someone crying and screaming, 'Don't, don't beat me.' I jumped up. But I couldn't see anything. And then it was over. I could still hear the plaintive, whimpering sobs."

A young transvestite had been thrown into a cell with other prisoners, who had beaten him up. "The thing that was so horrible about it is that no one went to help him," Perry continued. "The police just ignored him. It was the kind of indirect brutality that really galls me. They did nothing to him, but they refused to help him."[4]

I cringed again as I read Perry's indictment of the heterosexual Christian church. There was enough truth in the indictments that I could not ignore them.

He had been a pastor for a number of years when he discovered that he was gay. He told his superior—and was immediately put out of the pastorate. "Not once did they say, 'Can we pray for you?'—nothing except, 'How quick can you get out of town?' . . . How could the church not pray for me? I felt they had let me down."[5]

In another place he wrote, "Most organized religions have been no more helpful to us than an empty well, to which we have all returned again and again in some kind of forlorn spirit of hope. We who committed ourselves to a homosexual existence grew gradually to accept a feeling that God did not care about us."[6]

After he had been put out of his denomination and had broken up his marriage, he spent a considerable period of time trying to put his life together again, finally trying to commit suicide. Slowly the idea grew upon him that the Lord was leading him to start a church for homosexual people. It was not that he had any quarrel with existing churches; it was they who did not seem to want him. "My church was founded," he said, "because homosexuals simply didn't have any other place to go."[7]

When he began to share his dream of a gay church with other gay men and women, he wrote:

> Some told me to forget it, adding that most gays had made their peace with themselves, and that peace didn't include religion. I knew, then, how hard the job would be. We had gone through generations, even centuries, of that awful conviction that if you were a homosexual you could not be a child of God; you could not be a Christian. I was really shoveling sand against the tide to get started.[8]

One of the things about the book that really unsettled me was Perry's firm belief throughout the book that God was leading him to found the church and to fight for civil rights for gays. His whole approach was often very close to the way things were done at the Community of the Resurrection.

For example, in the early days of the Metropolitan Community Church they were worshiping in the Encore Theater but had already purchased an old church building that needed extensive remodeling. In order to have a building fund, Perry announced one Sunday that the next Sunday they would take an offering for the fund, and he set a goal of ten thousand dollars. During the week Perry fasted and prayed. The next Sunday he brought a twenty-gallon trash can to the service to collect the donations. The offering exceeded the ten-thousand-dollar goal.[9]

Another time when Perry was staging a sit-in for civil rights for gays, he again resorted to fasting and prayer.[10] When he marched to Sacramento to present his case to the state legislature, he did it with fasting and prayer.[11]

Because of the positive outcome in these cases, Perry interpreted the results as indications of God's blessing and approval of his actions. It was the same conclusion the members at the Community of the Resurrection would have made under similar circumstances, except . . . except I was still hung up on the question of whether God would respond as freely to a homosexual person's prayer and fasting as to a heterosexual's. I was ashamed of myself. My head agreed with what Perry was saying; my emotions were more unruly.

Other statements in the book bothered me for different reasons. I had reservations about the slogans "Gay is good," "Gay is proud," "Gay is just as good as straight." And what about the inference that God created the homosexual as he is and that therefore it would be a sin for him to change? What about the unquestioned assumption that sex is where you find it, with no moral dimension attached?

I couldn't agree with these sweeping generalities, but neither could I agree with the old stereotypes concerning homosexuals. I had fallen off the old bandwagon on which I had ridden, but I had reservations about the new one that was passing before my eyes.

I began to realize that it was time for me to venture out of my narrow little backwater and come to grips with the matter of homosexuality on a larger scale.

17

Sinner
or Victim?

I soon discovered that if one wants to find out about homosexuality, there is no lack of reading matter. Hundreds upon hundreds of books, fiction and nonfiction, and thousands upon thousands of articles have been published on the subject.

Often, I found, the books and articles disagreed. There was no unanimity of view. In addition, the credos of one decade seemed to be outmoded in the next, superseded by knowledge derived from better-conceived and more precise investigations and experiments.

As I began to read, I became aware of my enormous ignorance about almost every aspect of homosexuality. I had had no idea, for instance, of the actual number of persons living as homosexuals.

A widely quoted rule of thumb is that approximately 10 percent of any population is homosexual. In reality, I learned, probably nearer 5 percent of the population is exclusively homosexual throughout life, though one third of the population has had some homosexual experience.[1] This would mean that among the million persons living in the greater metropolitan area of Minneapolis and St. Paul, fifty thousand or more are gay or lesbian.

I was stunned. I would have guessed perhaps a thousand gay men and several hundred lesbians!

Another elementary fact of which I became aware as I read is that heterosexuality is not spotlessly clean and homosexuality unrelievedly soiled. If I had stopped to give even the most superficial thought to the matter, I would have realized that the umbrella of heterosexuality includes many spokes. It does not refer only to marriage and lifelong fidelity between a man and a woman. Adultery, fornication, divorce, promiscuity, prostitution, sadomasochism, rape, incest, and child molestation are other less savory aspects of the heterosexual orientation. The fact that a person is heterosexual guarantees nothing about him or her except the preference for a sexual partner of the opposite sex. I had never thought about heterosexuality in this light before. I had always assumed that heterosexuality was good, homosexuality bad.

Similarly, a statement about a person's homosexuality guarantees nothing about him or her except the preference for a sexual partner of the same sex. Beyond that, the umbrella of homosexuality includes a great variety of behaviors, some healthy and constructive, some pathological and destructive. I began to understand that there is no such person as a "typical" homosexual man or woman, any more than one can find a "typical" heterosexual man or woman.

As I read, I came to understand that the term homosexual is a simple adjective meaning "the same sex." The prefix *homo* does not come from the Latin word for man, but from the Greek word meaning "same." Any sexual behavior that deals with the same sex could therefore be termed homosexual.[2] During childhood there may be a period of experimentation between members of the same sex, behavior which usually passes as the child becomes older. Adolescence may bring with it a period of confusion about one's sexual identity. Again, there may be experimentation, perhaps with accompanying feelings of guilt and fear. In sexually segregated situations, such as prison or military service, normally heterosexual persons may turn to homosexual acts because the opportunity for these is available but heterosexual opportunities are not.

None of these homosexual acts necessarily means that a person has a homosexual orientation to life. The two may be, and often are, quite separate and distinct. The act may indicate experimentation, confusion, availability. A homosexual orientation to life, however, indicates a much deeper and all-inclusive idea about oneself and the behavior or patterns of relationship that carry out this idea.[3]

Once I had asked Eric when he had first realized he was gay.

"I always knew I was different from other people," he had said. "In high school, girls just didn't turn me on. When I got through my freshman year in college with a whole different crop of girls and realized that none of them turned me on either, I began to see where things were heading and that I had better do something about it."

"Did any of the fellows in high school interest you?" I had asked, repelled by my own question but feeling the need to ask it anyway.

"Yeah," he had replied, "Barry Z. and Woody and a couple others. I didn't do anything about it."

It was impossible for me to understand how a man could look at another man (or a woman at another woman) and feel sexual arousal, but it was not an arguable matter. Eric obviously had not made a decision about who would arouse him sexually and who would not. What had happened had simply happened. It was a fact he eventually had had to deal with.

The choice lay not in who would arouse him but in whether or not he was going to enter into a homosexual relationship (or relationships) or remain celibate. Perhaps even that was less a choice than one might suppose. Dr. Charles Socarides writes of persons who "repeatedly and out of inner necessity engage in sexual acts with partners of the same sex." Contrary to popular belief, he says, these people have "no choice."[4]

Morton Kelsey writes that "homosexuality is empowered with the full energy of the reproductive instinct and therefore falls into the same category with regard to its potency as the drive for food and self-preservation. It has deep unconscious roots and takes heroic strength to control."[5]

As I read, I saw that different people had differing ideas about the origins of homosexuality.

The general public has tended to be very inconsistent. Seventy-one percent think of homosexuality as an illness, yet more than half of these people want all evidence of this illness to be punished![6]

The majority of writers whose books I read put forth the conclusion I had arrived at by observing Eric's "family configurations"—Tom's and my relationship, his and my relationship to Eric, the relationships of our parents and of our grandparents. Homosexuality is the result of the way the child responds to the facts of his or her own particular environment. Each one phrased it differently, but it meant essentially the same thing.

Many Christian writers saw it as a deliberate, purposeful choice of sin, although they did acknowledge that those who are homosexual had been damaged during childhood by their home environment and that this damage had contributed to their homosexual orientation.

Other religion-oriented persons saw homosexuality as demon possession. This was what Paul Sundstrom believed. It was also indicated in an article in *New Wine* magazine that said, "There is a quality in the very nature of homosexuality that links it with the perverted rebellion of Satan and the demonic spirits."[7]

On the opposite side of the fence, many gay persons believe that they are "born that way." The religion-oriented ones often say that God created homosexuals and homosexuality and even go so far as to say that it would be a sin to change.

At first this was an idea I resisted vigorously. I could see how persons growing up in an environment that bent them in the direction of homosexuality would suppose that they were born that way. Every child tends to accept his or her experiences as the norm for all people. But that God *created* homosexuals and homosexuality I could not accept.

I had pretty well gotten my ideas about homosexuality in order when I received a jolt that made me rethink my entire stock of premises. Through a younger friend who was studying child psychology at the university, I learned of a book by John Money and Anke A. Ehrhardt entitled *Man and Woman, Boy and Girl.* The book provided a lot of new possibilities for me to consider.

The first page of *Man and Woman, Boy and Girl* demolished the neat structure I had put together.

> In the theory of psychosexual differentiation, it is now out-moded to juxtapose nature versus nurture, the genetic versus the environmental, the innate versus the acquired, the biological versus the psychological, or the instinctive versus the learned. . . . The basic proposition should not be a dichotomization of genetics and environment, but their interaction.[8]

Homosexuality, I had thought, is the result of the way the child responds to the facts of his or her own particular environment. This statement took on a totally new meaning as I plowed my way through Money's and Ehrhardt's book. At every juncture of the child's development there seemed to be a thousand interacting influences. These influences began not at the moment of birth but at the moment of conception and appeared to be incredibly complex at every stage.

The first and most obvious place where the dislocation of normal development may occur is in the selection of the sex chromosomes within the fertilized ova. Generally in homosexuality there is nothing so definitive involved as chromosome abnormalities. The dislocation, if there is one, is of a much less definite nature. For example, the embryo and then the fetus may be influenced by much that goes on in the mother's body:

"a deficiency or excess of maternal hormone, viral invasion, intrauterine trauma, nutritional deficiency or toxicity, and so forth."[9]

The hormones the fetus produces for himself or herself also play a role in the child's sexual development. These may be influenced very subtly by many seemingly unrelated occurrences. The fetus is not developing in an impersonal environment. He or she is living inside a human being who is subject to many internal and external stresses. What happens to the fetus when the mother is very angry, depressed, chronically under stress, chronically overtired? What about the influence of medications, tobacco, and alcohol?

The events of a particular birth can exert an influence upon the child, not only physiologically but quite possibly emotionally as well. The fact that we do not seem to remember our birth does not mean that impressions were not recorded somewhere in our being. Physical trauma can influence emotions, and emotional trauma can trigger physical responses. The two may be like interlocking spirals, impossible to separate and consider apart from each other.

From the moment of birth onward, external influences are bombarding the baby, colliding with his or her genetic inheritance, molding and shaping it to a greater or lesser degree, just as the genetic inheritance is exerting an influence on the external environment.

It was utterly, incredibly mind-boggling. What effect might my muddled perceptions of masculinity and femininity have had upon Eric? There was no way, of course, that I could ever know. Whatever I might think would remain forever conjecture.

Suppose, however, that I perceived the male (as my mother had seemed to do) as both the ultimate threat and the ultimate savior. Unintentionally, her femaleness had been subtly devalued by her widowed mother as the maleness of her brother, in the absence of the dead father, was overvalued. Added to that was her unconscious feeling of rejection by the dead father. At her very young age, how could she know he had not left her and gone away forever because she was such a bad little girl? Her brother had been born at about the same time, displacing her as the center of the family. No wonder she saw the male as a threat to herself, an enemy. Mother never knew any of this consciously, but both Meg and I had perceived the message clearly.

In addition to being the enemy, however, the male was also the savior. At the time Mother was growing up, it was almost imperative for a woman to marry. The man was the way to economic security. There were very few careers for women at that time; indeed, any job opportunities for women were quite limited.

I had grown up, therefore, receiving mixed signals from my mother concerning men. (I have often wondered what would have happened if she had had a son, and I have concluded that it was fortunate she didn't!)

What, I wondered now, had been the interaction of my *psyche* and my *soma*, my mind and my body, when my body became aware that the coming child was a male? My conscious mind had not known the sex of the child, but had my unconscious understood, through the language of hormones, what was taking place within my body? Had my body, in an effort at conquering the enemy, produced more than the normal amount of female hormones? Whatever may have happened had not been sufficient to produce any physical ambiguities in Eric. There was no problem at birth in determining the sex to which he belonged.

But there are "certain patterns of organization in the brain" that are influenced prenatally by the hormone secretions of the fetus.[10] Was it possible that these might have been organized a little bit differently because of unconscious physical reactions on my part that perhaps had triggered a difference in fetal hormones? I had no way of knowing, no way of ever finding out. I didn't even know if it was a scientifically valid supposition. But it seemed to me that it might be a possibility.

It was not something over which I could feel guilty. If I had made a decision that I was going to cause great difficulties in life for my son, I could reasonably feel guilty. I had to acknowledge, when I thought about it in this light, that neither had Mother deliberately set out to make life as difficult for me as she could.

I began to see that if each person enters life with a particular set of physical and mental "givens," which are shaped by the individual circumstances of his or her inheritance, it is no wonder that gays and lesbians have felt that God made them that way. In an existential way, God has. I could not believe, however, that homosexuality had been God's ideal plan for the world when God created it.

If, as a reading of *Man and Woman, Boy and Girl* seemed to indicate, one's entire sexual adjustment in life could be influenced, greatly or less greatly, by an uncounted multitude of factors beyond anyone's conscious control, what did this have to do with the simple, unequivocal statements in the Bible that homosexuality is an abomination and that no homosexual person would inherit the kingdom of God? Was a person condemned because of factors over which he or she had no control?

The answer to that question, it seemed to me, had to be a resounding no!

What was the meaning, then, of biblical statements about homosexuality? The verse in Leviticus, for example, "If a man lies with a male as with a woman, both of them have committed an abomination; they shall be put to death, their blood is upon them,"[11] seemed to me to be a rather direct, concise statement. It did not readily lend itself to more than one interpretation.

And what about the story of Sodom and Gomorrah? Was it not obvious that God had destroyed the cities because of their practice of homosexuality? And what about Paul's statements concerning homosexuality? If they were not dependable and true, would that make the whole Bible false?

If the Bible is, as I believed, "without error in all that it affirms,"[12] and if homosexuality is the result of forces over which a person has little or no control, the gay person lives in an impossible bind. God, it would seem, had left the gay and the lesbian in a limbo from which there is no exit.

18

New Paths Through the Desert

If I have learned anything in the course of the last ten or fifteen years of my life, it is that a seeming impasse can be God's opportunity for opening new paths through the desert.

For more than a year I wrestled with the problem of the inerrancy of scripture versus what I had learned about possible causes of homosexuality. If the Bible was not "without error in all that it affirms, and the only infallible rule of faith and practice," did this mean that nothing in the Bible is true? Where would one draw the line between what is true and what is not true? Was it all or nothing? Or was there some tenable middle ground?

Out of that year of struggle, of reading and studying and thinking and praying, has emerged a faith upon which I can take a firm stand, a faith that I believe is spiritually as well as intellectually sound. In the process God seemed to throw open doors in all directions. It was as if I had come out of a small, cramped, dark room into a limitless garden with marvelous vistas. Light, freedom, air were all around me; and all the time that I had supposed God was only in that dark, cramped room, God had been out here, waiting for me to discover the vast world created and intended for me and all God's other children to enjoy.

One of my first realizations was that the Bible may well be inerrant. It may have in it exactly what God intended it should. But our interpretations of what it is saying may be often very errant. Those who say, "The Bible is without error in all that it affirms" are really saying that *their interpretation of what the Bible is saying* is without error.

The Bible is not a simple piece of literature which easily yields up its meaning. If someone put a piece of writing from 1500 B.C. into your hands and asked you to read and apply it to your present-day life, you would laugh in that person's face. "How can that have any relation to my life in the twentieth century?" you would ask. It would be a thoroughly legitimate question.

"But," the inerrancy people say, "God was directing what should be written, and therefore the Bible contains timeless truth."

The key word in that statement is contains. The message of one book of the Bible may be very different from that of another book. Only as we can see the place of each book in the total impact of the Bible will we begin to have an understanding of what the real message of an individual book may be.

Some church bodies have understood that the Bible is not offering the same kind of guidance in every verse. One Protestant church puts it this way: "I do believe the Holy Scriptures of the Old and New Testaments to be the Word of God, and to contain all things necessary to salvation."[1] Another has said, "I believe in the divine truths of the Holy Scripture."[2]

If we are going to understand what any fifteenth- or sixteenth-century B.C. manuscript may have to say to our day, we must search out its deeper meaning. If we try to transport its literal meaning across the centuries, it may very well not have anything at all to say to us.

This became clear to me one day when I was reading *Woman's*

Mysteries by M. Esther Harding. She was speaking about the taboos that surrounded menstruation and childbirth in primitive cultures. At the end of the lying-in period a woman had to be "disinfected, not surgically, but religiously."[3]

I remembered the instructions in the Bible concerning women who were menstruating or who had borne a child. The menstrual period was variously referred to as "sickness," "impurity," "uncleanness." After a woman had borne a male child, she was "unclean" for seven days, after which the child was circumcised. Then she continued "in the blood of her purifying" for thirty-three days. After she had borne a female child, she was "unclean" for two weeks and continued "in the blood of her purifying" for sixty-six days![4]

Here was an instruction in the Bible based on primitive cultural understandings which were common to all people of that period of the world's history. The idea that menstruation, a perfectly normal physiological occurrence which women cannot avoid, is "unclean" is not likely to receive much modern acceptance. And why, in the name of heaven, would bearing a child make a woman impure? She is doing only what nature programmed her to do! That it takes twice as long to "purify" a mother after the birth of a girl as after the birth of a boy is enough to incite today's liberated woman to some justifiably strong comments. We cannot transplant rules uncritically across thirty-five centuries.

If we cannot translate instructions concerning a woman's menstrual period and childbirth intact across the centuries, perhaps we cannot take over ancient ideas about homosexuality unquestioned into the present day. What did the writer of Leviticus understand the word homosexuality to mean? Was he writing of those who are *unable* to live heterosexually? Or was he viewing homosexuality in other lights?

I am no great student of biblical history. Nevertheless, by now I have knocked about enough in various books and articles to know that there were at least two uses of homosexuality in that era. One was as sacred prostitution in worshiping gods other than Jehovah. The other was the perpetrating of homosexual rape by conquering armies upon the conquered. It was a very graphic way of expressing the most extreme degree of contempt for the fallen foes. Sex in this context had nothing to do with normal sexual desire. It was purely a demonstration of dominance and hostility. Essentially the conquerors were using sex to demonstrate power. Conceivably they were saying, "You're nothing but a woman," and in those days women *were* nothing.

If either of these two types of homosexual practices is what the writer of Leviticus was condemning, of course it was an abomination to God for a number of legitimate reasons.

When I turned to the story of Sodom and Gomorrah, I began to realize that here again what the Bible seemed to be saying could differ considerably from what it actually was saying.

The story does not deal with a homosexual orientation to life. Obviously every last man in these two cities could not have had such an orientation or Lot would not have settled there. The story deals rather with the condemnation of homosexual rape.

There is the added, very important factor that this particular attempted homosexual rape, the ultimate put-down of that day, was to be perpetrated against the messengers of God. Thus the issues at Sodom and Gomorrah had nothing to do with an obligatory homosexual life orientation. They revolved, rather, around an attitude toward one's neighbors and toward God that was thoroughly vicious and depraved.

The Old Testament's condemnation of homosexuality must also be viewed from the standpoint of the rise of patriarchal life. There was a time in the development of the world when primitive man was not aware of his contribution to the creation of life. The woman's monthly cycle (and we need to remember that they did not have neat calendars to mark off months) seemed to correspond to the phases of the moon, and it was believed that a woman got herself with child by lying in the moonlight. In our scientific day and age, we can scarcely imagine what a primitive understanding of the world was like. The time that elapsed between intercourse and the swelling of a woman's body with pregnancy was far too long for primitive people to be able to make any connection.

Gradually somehow that connection was made. Man had a part in creating new life! The woman could not do it without the man! Suddenly the man had an importance he had not enjoyed before. He was the important one now. The woman needed him and the seed he could plant within her.

It is quite possible that this had implications for homosexuality. Men were not to squander precious male semen where it would not produce offspring, either in religious rites with male or female prostitutes, in homosexual rape to indicate one's loathing of the person raped, or in any other homosexual relationship. Male semen was needed in order to increase the population so that the tribe would not die out. In the history of the development of the Hebrew nation and its worship of a male deity, we see the rise of patriarchy and the clash with the worship of the Great Mother with its more primitive emphasis on matriarchal society.

It is no wonder modern Christians have such difficulty wading through much of the early part of the Old Testament. It seems to have little or no relationship to our present-day life except as we dive in and retrieve a verse or two here and there, such as "You shall not lie with a male as with a woman; it is an abomination."[5]

We do not retrieve the verses that deal with the woman's uncleanness during menstruation, a man's uncleanness after an emission of semen, instructions concerning a man's cutting his hair or shaving his beard, or instructions prohibiting the use of two different kinds of fiber in the same garment. We ignore the chapters and chapters of instructions concerning sacrifice, instructions for identifying and dealing with leprosy, and regulations concerning "clean" and "unclean" animals.

Many of these regulations had very practical implications for limiting the spread of disease in a day when the knowledge of the existence of bacteria lay three thousand or more years in the future. There were also symbolic implications. Some of these could tell us something about eternal or divine truths if we took the time and trouble to dig out the real meanings. We cannot glean these truths, however, from literal or superficial interpretations.

Paul's injunctions concerning homosexuality continue the prohibitions laid down in the Old Testament. In the passage in Romans, which is perhaps the most definitive one in the New Testament, Paul is clearly writing about idolatry. Pagan worship with sacred male and female prostitutes leads to his saying that, when they had

exchanged the glory of the immortal God for images resembling mortal man or birds or animals or reptiles . . . God gave them up . . . to the dishonoring of their bodies among themselves. . . . Their women exchanged natural relations for unnatural, and the men likewise gave up natural relations with women and were consumed with passion for one another, men committing shameless acts with men and receiving in their own persons the due penalty for their error.[6]

If we were to study the social and sexual history of the various cities and countries in Paul's day where he established churches, I believe we would begin to understand why he wrote as he did concerning homosexuality. He was referring to specific situations and specific practices, which his parishioners had perhaps only lately forsaken.

I do not believe we can read into his statements any idea that he knew there was such a thing as an obligatory homosexual orientation to life. If we adhered slavishly to the letter of the law as laid down by Paul, women could not speak in church, people would be reluctant to marry, and slavery would never have been outlawed.

Again, we need to understand those truths in holy scripture which are divine. It is not always easy to discern such truths. And we have to confess that different eras have often discerned divine truths differently. A glaring example of this is the total blindness of our early American forebears to the fact that slavery is an unmitigated evil. The Bible was in part culturally determined, just as our understanding of it is often influenced by the day in which we live.

Probably the most important statement the Bible makes about homosexuality is no statement at all. None of the four Gospel writers has recorded any sayings of Jesus concerning homosexuality. What is the meaning of this silence?

One would assume that if it had been a matter of overriding importance, Jesus would have had something to say about it. But it is all too easy to rush in and conjecture about this lack of mention. One may well end up drawing all sorts of spurious implications.

It seems to me that if we view the Bible as an ironbound wooden box, nailed together from stout timbers, which contains God and the rules for the world, we are going to run into no end of difficulties. If we try to attach scientific accuracy to biblical statements that were intended to be symbolic, we find ourselves in another kind of dilemma. If, however, we view the Bible as the record of how people perceived God through long ages, then we are beginning to get onto the right track. Certainly the God who is portrayed at some places in the Old Testament is far different from the God who is revealed in Jesus. This does not mean that God has changed through the ages. Only our understanding of God has changed.

The Bible is, first of all, a historical record of certain events that occurred at specific times. But that is only its outer meaning. In addition, it is also the record of humanity's inner symbolic and spiritual journey and thus lends itself to interpretation in psychological or inner terms.

One has only to read the myths of other early or primitive peoples to realize that many of these same stories appear in slightly different form in the Bible. It comes at first as a shock to realize that even the roles of Mary and Jesus appear over and over and over in primitive myth, certainly not as we understand them really to have been but veiled within the symbols of the Great Mother and her son, the Dying and Rising God. It is likewise a shock to realize that the symbolism of blood, the substitution of wine for blood, and the symbols of bread and wine are not exclusively Judaic or Christian. They appear in many other places and at many other times as well.

There has evidently been among all people everywhere and in every age some unconscious perception of the principles upon which God established the universe and the symbols that embody those principles. Both principles and symbols have been brought to their highest form, their highest meaning, in the Bible.

Morality is not, therefore, a matter of making everyone conform to outward laws. It is true that for thousands of years morality has usually meant just such a conformity. But as we look around today and see the conformity to outward laws in shambles all about us, it would seem that perhaps the time has come when God is indeed putting divine principles within the people, writing them upon their hearts instead of upon rule books.[7] Morality, we are discovering, must be a much more complex and demanding discipline than mere outward conformity. If God's principles do not begin to arise from within our lives because we *must* find a better way or perish, they will not arise at all.

The message that we drew from the Bible in past ages was that we ought to adhere strictly to the outer rules. With the understandings that psychology, and especially Carl Jung, have opened up to us, we are now beginning to perceive an additional inner dimension.

If, as it would seem, there are both genetic and psychological causes for homosexuality, then we cannot discount these as we try to interpret the Bible. Genesis may say, "Male and female created he them," but we know that every baby born is not clearly one sex or the other. If there are also psychological intersexes, what does the Christian church have to say to such people? The day of simplistic answers is over. We cannot rap out a pat rule and feel we have covered the situation.

It would seem to be evident that man and woman complete each other, both physically and emotionally, in a way that man and man, or woman and woman, do not. Yet if some people are born with a genetic/psychological orientation that does not allow them to enter into a heterosexual relationship, are they beyond the love of Christ? Can the church simply turn its back on the sexual anomalies of the world and ignore them?

If the church does say, "Jesus loves gays and lesbians," can its further message to them be only that because they can't live out their sexual lives in the normal way, they cannot have any sexual lives at all? If the message to heterosexual persons was, "In order to enter the kingdom of God you have to forego all sexual life, " I wonder how many heterosexual people would choose to enter the kingdom!

This is not an easy matter. Perhaps the same standards that apply to the highest heterosexual relationships need to be applied to homosexual relationships as well. There are many principles of relationship that apply to any two people who may live together and share their lives, whether there is any sexual relationship or not. Norman Pittenger has argued persuasively that the church should help the homosexual person be the best person he or she can be.[8]

Perhaps the issue of which gender is the recipient of any one person's love, sexual and otherwise, is not as important as the quality of the relationship. Is it better to be a wife-abusing heterosexual man or a homosexual man or woman who has a genuine love and respect for his or her partner of the same sex?

Is it possible that the church has come as far as the old path of outward rules will take it? New paths must then be found. And they will be discovered as we look at what science is demonstrating to be reasonably true and bring the deeper meanings of the Bible to bear upon the new knowledge.

This may mean a new searching for the nuggets of gold—the divine truths, those things necessary for salvation—that are contained in God's word. This may seem a risky venture to those who feel more comfortable with the known boundaries of definite rules. It may even seem to them that we are throwing out the word of God in favor of the word of science. It is well to remember, however, that the church initially rejected Copernicus' and Galileo's discovery that the earth revolves around the sun, not vice versa. God's truth is sometimes so much greater than we want to allow it to be.

Who knows? Perhaps God is confronting the church with the present crisis over homosexuality not in order to demolish the church but because God is saying, "Grow or die." Our impasse, or extremity, may be nothing more than God's offering us a new and life-giving opportunity to expand our understanding of the ancient scriptures.

19

Integrating
the Wolf

The sun was shining in a blue summer sky decked with spun-sugar clouds. The countryside rushing past my car was a patchwork of fields of lush green tobacco and ripe golden grain.

I was driving the back roads of southern Wisconsin on my way to meet a woman I did not know. As my car went uphill and down, around sharp bends and curves, I thought about the coming interview.

Hans had recently sent me an article written by a woman named Peggy Way. In the early 1960s, when she was working with the Chicago City Missionary Society, there was an attempt to establish dialogue between the church and the homophile community. Since no one else on the staff was interested in this venture, she was assigned to the weekend retreat. She took along her husband and their two small children.

Several years later, when she was on the faculty of the Urban Training Center in Chicago, she worked on some of the first clergy-lay dialogues dealing with homosexuality. Later she was invited to join the board of Mattachine Midwest, a homophile group, and she served in this capacity for six years. More recently she had spent six years as a pastoral counselor, becoming known as one to whom gays—both men and women—could come.

It was not her qualifications, though they were impressive, that had prompted me to write to her asking for an interview. It was the fact that, though heterosexual and monogamous, she seemed to understand thoroughly both gay and straight feelings on the highly sensitive and explosive issue of homosexuality. Without amalgamating them, she seemed to be able to knit the two warring strands together into some kind of sensible pattern. I wanted to meet this woman!

One of the points in her article that had struck me was that frequently both heterosexual and homosexual persons fall into the trap of seeing the homosexual orientation to life as the first, and therefore by implication the most important, thing we can say about a person.[1]

Some time before reading Ms. Way's article I had come across this statement by Dr. Lawrence Hatterer: "The homosexual does not exist. Only people who fantasy, feel, and act homosexually exist. Homosexual life styles and subcultures exist."[2] These words had puzzled me. Of course homosexuals existed, I had thought. Now I realized Dr. Hatterer had been saying that homosexuals are first of all *persons*, and that the definitive statement about a person is usually not a description of his or her sexuality. That is only one component of many.

Alan W. Jones, who works with priests preparing for ordination, put the idea this way: "The question is: 'Am I a Christian who happens to be a homosexual/heterosexual?' or 'Am I a homosexual/heterosexual who happens to be a Christian?' "[3]

As a culture we have worked (and are still working) our way through accepting blacks, American Indians, Hispanics, and women as persons first, and only secondarily, if at all, as belonging to a specific category. Would it be possible to do this with gays?

There is a difference, of course, between these other categories and the homosexual person. There is always the possibility, at least in theory if often not in probability, that a homosexual orientation may be altered and become mainly heterosexual, while it is impossible to change one's color, ethnic stock, or sex (except under extreme circumstances in this last case).

Precisely because the general public sees homosexuality as more or less a matter of choice, acceptance of the gay person becomes more difficult.

"The deviant—sexual, religious or political—is always seen as stabbing at his community's vitals by disregarding its self-defining principles," Arno Karlen has written. "Those who hold the dominant view tend to see him as part of the conspiracy or hostile clique out to destroy the most cherished values, and to control society as society wants to control him."[4]

He points out that sexual regulation is not an arbitrary decree by one element in society. It is a reflection of the norms in all that society's institutions—religion, civil law, ethical values, customs, humor, folkways, art.

For this reason throughout history the homosexual person has always been the underdog in one way or another. In the Middle Ages homosexuality was termed "the nameless crime not fit to be named by Christians." It was punished in England by burning, drowning, hanging, or being buried alive. In Spain in the thirteenth century the penalty was to be castrated and then stoned to death. Other places on the continent there are records of executions at the stake for homosexuality.[5]

This type of punishment continued through the Renaissance into Puritan times and the coming to the New World. The witch-hunts which were carried on throughout this period were due primarily to the witches' supposed traffic (largely sexual) with the devil, but at least part of their actions was associated with homosexuality.

The time finally came when prison was substituted for the death penalty for homosexuality. To the present day there are laws in the United States that can put a homosexual in jail for five, ten, or twenty years, or even for life.[6] There are also laws against sodomy in many states and communities. Though they are generally used only in cases of forced sodomy, the possibility exists that not only consenting homosexual persons could find themselves in jail because of their actions but heterosexual married couples could as well.

The whole subject of social control of homosexuality is neither a small nor a light matter for heterosexual or homosexual society. The roots of the whole matter extend deep into the personal and collective unconscious. We say and do things as individuals or as groups, not because of rational objective decisions but because forces buried in our unconscious, of which we are unaware, move us this way or that.

This became apparent during Anita Bryant's crusade in Dade County, Florida, for the repeal of an ordinance prohibiting discrimination against gays. During that campaign gays were referred to as "human garbage."[7] It was said that "so-called gay folks [would] as soon kill you as look at you" and that "we are facing the Devil himself in these homosexuals."[8] Bumper stickers surfaced with the appalling slogan "Kill a queer for Christ."[9] Obviously these were frenzied cries rooted in ignorance and desperate fear.

Until psychology and genetic research appeared on the scene, there was no possible way to understand the causes of homosexuality except as willful and perverse choice. In religious terms this was translated at best into choosing to sin. At worst, it was seen as an involvement directly inspired by Satan.

Homosexuality seemed to challenge the very fabric of life, the most deeply rooted pattern of sexuality necessary for the survival of the race. Even though we now have at least some rudimentary indications of possible causes of homosexuality, the heritage of fear and misunderstanding that has been built up over thousands of years is not dissipated easily or quickly.

An article in *Time* summed up the problem: "In the end,

homosexuals are likely to get full rights only when—and if—the public perceives that they are no threat to that part of society's established value system that is rooted in heterosexuality."[10]

There is in each one of us, and thus in the collective psyche, a rejected side of ourselves, part of our total personality that we do not want to face and that is therefore hidden within our unconscious, unrecognized and forgotten. Whatever homosexual feelings or inclinations we may have—and every child goes through a stage when he or she identifies strongly with his/her own sex and regards the opposite sex with distaste—are generally relegated to this unremembered basement of our consciousness. In addition, there may be in our unconscious many confusions surrounding what we perceive as masculine and feminine.

When the subject of homosexuality comes up, in whatever context, our reaction is likely to be one of fear or distaste. The unsuspected prisoner in our psyche has reacted to the word or the situation in one way or another, giving us a feeling of dis-ease. Without understanding the cause of this feeling, we simply know that anything related to homosexuality causes us discomfort, and we respond accordingly, "Stamp it out. Put it down. Keep it under lock and key." At the least, "Ignore it."

The truth is that we cannot stamp it out. We can put it down or, to an extent, try to keep it under lock and key. Many times we can ignore it. None of these methods, however, is really dealing with the Thing locked away in our unconscious. The time comes when the issue of homosexuality in civil, social, or religious situations again arises, and we are called on to make some sort of decision.

Too often we project our horror of this part of ourselves out onto other people. Undoubtedly this is why supposedly sane, sophisticated, twentieth-century persons could sink to the level of a seventeenth-century witch-hunt as they did in Dade County; it is also why, more recently, ordinances banning discrimination against gays have been suffering defeat at the polls. The same thing happened, on a far larger and more horrifying scale, when the superrace of Nazis projected their flaws upon the hapless Jews.[11] For centuries, too, whites have projected their own feared and unwanted characteristics onto blacks.

Bringing a rejected side of ourselves up into the light and seeking to deal with it constructively is not a simple or easy business. It is not easy to integrate some part of ourselves that may seem to us like a dangerous inner wolf, prowling on the outskirts of our safe, tidy, outer life.

When, however, the rejected side "is given dignity and status it is no longer the adversary," Robert Johnson writes in *He!* "It is an adversary only when it is excluded. . . . It is a general principle that anything that is rejected from one's psyche becomes hostile. If one understands this, one is well on the way to knowing what to do about it."[12]

How to give dignity and status is the crucial question.

It seemed to me that Peggy Way might be very helpful in this regard.

She welcomed me into a living room with cartons stacked in various corners. The family was in the throes of moving to a new city because of new jobs for both Peggy and her husband, Bill. Both of them, I discovered, had their master's degrees in social work, and both were ordained ministers.

Peggy and I sat down for a concentrated chat.

From reading her article several times, I was aware that she was as sensitive to the feelings and fears of heterosexual people as she was to those of gays and that she met issues not on the basis of what a person *ought* to feel but on the recognition of the real gut reactions of each side. When these had been brought into the open and acknowledged, the way was opened for dialogue that could be helpful.

I had come with several questions. "What about gays, either men or women, teaching children and dealing with young people?" I asked for an opener. It was the issue around which the Dade County fight, and subsequent fights in other cities, had revolved.

"I have no problems with it myself," she answered. "If I were in a position to hire a known homosexual person for a teaching job, or if I were a Sunday school superintendent selecting a Sunday school teacher, I would make sure I had a clear understanding with the person beforehand that their homosexual preference of lifestyle had no place in the classroom. It is illegal in many places to do this, but I would do it anyway. It would clear the air for both the person I was hiring and myself. We would each know where the other stood."

It sounded simple and easy when she said it. I knew, however, that she had come to this place where she could deal forthrightly and confidently with such a situation because she had faced and worked through an awareness and an acceptance of her own sexuality. She had also, in the most emotionally charged situation anyone could devise, tested her theories about allowing gays to be in contact with young people.

"Another mild crisis in my own pilgrimage [came] when I transferred my counseling practice to my home, so that I had a continual succession of homosexual persons having coffee with me, *meeting my children*," she had written. Her principles had developed from real situations, honestly faced, lived and worked through, rather than from bloodless, abstract theories of what one "ought" to do in a given situation. Her words carried weight because she'd been through it on the gut level.

Some months later an article in a Minneapolis newspaper dealt with the same question about gay teachers that I put to Peggy that afternoon. " 'We don't advocate our sexuality any more than we advocate a particular religion, political ideology, or any other personal matter,' " a gay teacher in Minneapolis was quoted as saying. " 'We'd be fired for that, with or without a civil rights law.'

" 'A teacher is hired to teach—not to talk about his or her sex life,' " the article continued, quoting a Minneapolis member of the National Gay Task Force. " 'Gay teachers are as committed to this standard of professionalism as are other teachers. Any teachers who violate this standard can and should be removed for misconduct.' "[13]

It seemed to me to be such a sensible, obvious approach to the question that I wondered why I had not understood this years before.

Another question that I had jotted down for my interview with Peggy was, what about the gay community's request that "marriages" be performed for persons of the same sex? Without hesitation she answered, "I would never perform a homosexual marriage. Marriage is a religious and social institution that carries too much weight and too much symbolism to try to twist it into something it was never meant to be."

I knew she was referring not only to the verses in Genesis where God created the sexual difference, joined it together, and saw that it was good but also to the verses later in the Bible that see marriage as a reflection of the relationship between Christ and the church.[14]

"I would be very open to and very much interested in developing services of commitment for homosexual couples, or covenanting services for them," she went on. "There is no reason that the church cannot develop new rituals to meet new needs. Gay persons who value committed relationships have no way at present to indicate publicly such a pledge of faithfulness to a chosen partner. A good bit of gay culture—particularly among men and in urban areas—focuses around the bars, drinking, and the stimulation of genital sexuality. One cause, of course, is the forced exclusion of gays from the broader culture and the consequent need they feel for places where they need not pretend. Obviously, this creates an atmosphere not supportive of fidelity.

"The consequence of all this is that gay persons concerned about fidelity, about relating genital expression to life commitment, frequently find no support—either from the gay community or from the straight community which views homosexual activity itself as immoral. And the church, in its concern for morality, turns away from these moral hungers and concerns!"

We talked then about the church and its relationship to the homosexual community.

"One of the primary difficulties at present," Peggy said, "is that because the church generally has rejected the gay community in its entirety, the church is in no position to offer any sort of comment or critique to the gay community on any subject. Any suggestions, comments, criticism, or ideas that the church may offer are simply written off in the gay community because for centuries, and even today, the church has blanketly condemned homosexual persons and homosexuality."

There it was again, that approach which was so simple and so sensible that it seemed almost self-evident. Why had I failed to see what now seemed very obvious? More important, why had church leadership generally failed to grasp these principles?

"There are a lot of excesses in the gay rights movement," she went on, "things that are guaranteed to antagonize straights or that just aren't very smart."

"I know," I said feelingly, thinking of gay activists who behaved irresponsibly and have been the gay rights movement's own worst enemies. Floats in gay rights parades with shrieking drag queens, young men dripping with chains, and representations of giant phallic symbols could hardly impress the straight community with the wisdom and maturity of the gay community. Young men throwing cream pies at public figures who opposed homosexual rights had contributed nothing useful to gay-straight dialogue. It might have been great fun while these things were going on, I thought, but the damage to the real issues of gay rights was hardly worth the price.

"Whenever I can," Peggy was saying, "I suggest to the gay community that it monitor itself and deal with excesses or patterns of behavior that don't make sense in anyone's language, gay or straight."

There it was again, that wisdom which looked at an action and asked, first of all, "Does it make rational sense?" The criterion was not, "Is it gay or straight?" The standard was: "Is it useful? Is it helpful? Does it tear down or build up the whole fabric of society, not just the heterosexual or the homosexual community?" The standards were valid, no matter to which side they were applied, because in the end both sides were parts of the whole.

I drove back to my motel marveling.

If the church through the centuries had been able to come to grips with many of its problems in such a courageous and intelligent way, how many "holy wars," how much figurative and literal bloodshed could have been avoided!

20

Morning
of Joy

Several years have passed since that fateful weekend visit to
Chicago and Barbara's early-morning phone call. They marked
a crucial turning point in my life. Nothing has been the same for
me since then. Nothing can ever be the same again. Life has
been divided into "before" and "after"—"before I learned
about Eric" and "after I learned about Eric." There is no way I
can go back.

Many times since that weekend I have wondered why I had
that moment of déjà vu in the coal mine at the Museum of
Science and Industry.

At the time, the experience seemed to say to me, "God has his
hand on the events of your life, even in this moment of
anguish." But why had I not dreamed of the darkened living
room of Hans's and Emily's apartment and the phone ringing at
one-thirty in the morning? Why not some other scene from that
weekend? Why was the moment in the coal mine more important than any of the other moments?

A dozen or more years ago I was in the psychiatric ward of a
hospital five hundred miles from the town where we were then

living. I had needed to return to my first psychiatrist in order to try to explore a frightening chasm that had suddenly opened before me in the dimness of my unconscious mind.

In spite of the heavy, painful psychic burden I was carrying, I enjoyed the interlude. I was free of household chores, free of the responsibility of the children. Except for the time each morning when I talked with Dr. Liggett, I was free to do as I pleased.

I went down to the occupational therapy room, but the neat little craft kits and the paint-by-number things did not appeal to me. I wanted finger paints. Some intuitive awareness must have told me that when my hands came into direct contact with the paints and the paper, something deep within me could be transferred to the paper.

The sisters in occupational therapy provided me with the paints and a roll of shelf paper. One of the other patients, a woman named Sally, and I went to it, covering sheet after sheet of shelf paper with crude, strongly colored creations. The pictures that I most clearly remember making were all dark. For some reason, which I did not understand at the time, I was obsessed with painting coal mines.

The unconscious mind is a marvelous creation. Instead of serving up words to tell us about ourselves and our relationship to the world and the universe, it serves up pictures. As I finally discovered when I began digging within myself under Lee's guidance, I had a coal mine of solidified anger within myself.

Why had I envisioned the mock coal mine rather than some other scene from that momentous weekend? How could my unconscious mind have had this scene available before it actually took place?

I have no clear answers to these questions. I do know that the conscious mind operates in a world that is governed and limited by space and time, by what we can touch and taste and see and feel and measure. But our unconscious mind is always in touch with timeless, intangible reality. Because it operates outside the limitations of time, we are sometimes able to glimpse for a moment something that lies ahead.

The unconscious world and the conscious are indissolubly linked. They influence each other; but the wellsprings of life proceed from the unconscious. When we become conscious of what is hidden within our unconscious mind, we begin to find a harmony in life which is never possible when we deal only with the conscious mind and leave the unconscious to its own devices.

The secret of the abundant life of which Jesus spoke, it seems to me, lies in the integration of the unconscious with the conscious. It is a curious fact that as we become aware of our "dark side," those unpleasant parts of ourselves that have been repressed into our unconscious minds, we become more whole because we become more complete.

To be whole means to be perfect not in the sense of being without flaw but in the sense of being complete. We know not only our heights but our depths as well. The missing information, which we somehow knew all the time was there, has been transferred into consciousness. There is a peace that comes when we know the whole truth about ourselves.

When there is a huge backlog of a particular emotion buried in our unconscious, we are likely to be informed of this through recurring images in dreams. Our unconscious continues to send us frantic signals, whether we are able to interpret these signals or not.

Over a period of years, apparently, I had been receiving signals about coal mines. At last, at a moment of the most crucial importance in my life, I received the signal in a way I could hardly ignore.

Strangely, as I plunged into the depths of the darkness within me, as I have come to know all those despised parts of myself which before I had suppressed and ignored, I have found the abundance of life that Jesus talked about. Out of my struggle to come to terms with all my unacknowledged anger, out of the struggle to come to terms with the confusion of masculine and feminine elements within my psyche, has come healing. To a much greater extent than ever before, I am whole.

I wonder if there is a correlation between the microcosm of

my experience and the whole matter of homosexuality in our society. A sentence in Morton Kelsey's *Myth, History and Faith* seems to sum up my experience: "How often the healing of our brokenness comes only from this rejected part of ourselves, from some part of the unconscious from which we have been separated."[1] Is it possible that this sentence could apply to collective as well as individual brokenness? Can it be that the despised condition of homosexuality may yet be an avenue by which society can find wholeness?

Please do not misunderstand what I am saying when I write that. I certainly do not mean anything as mindless as that healing will come as more people become gay!

Recently I was in a group with a gay priest. I was trying to explain to him why I believe Eric is homosexual. He replied by offering his explanation of why he is gay: "I believe that my family needed someone to fill that particular slot. Not that they knew they needed someone to be gay. But they did. And without my knowing I was volunteering, I did. I said, in effect, 'I'll fill that slot for you.' "

Dr. Charles Silverstein has expressed this same idea when he writes:

> Members of a family most often help each other in ways they do not understand. Family members often have the ability to sense the others' private needs although these are never discussed. Family members play roles that help maintain the psychological stability of the others, no matter what the risks to themselves.[2]

So it may be in the human family. In order for heterosexuality to have existed as a strong force through the ages, there have been those who have carried the opposite side of the coin, with all its attendant pain and scorn. For reasons we do not fully understand, they have been the bearers of our darkness, our despised side.

If we can be brave enough to look beyond our knee-jerk reactions of fear, prejudice, and distaste for homosexuality; if we can allow homosexuality to surface within society without the reflex response of trying to stamp it out or, at the very least, to force it back underground—if we dare these things, perhaps we shall discover something important about the whole realm of sexuality. From time immemorial there have been homosexual members of the human family. Until now we have ignored whatever message their existence may have had for the entire family of humankind.

I hope that perhaps the time has come to find out what that message is.

*　　*　　*　　*

Not long ago I was worshiping with what is probably an almost totally gay congregation. There were several people in that congregation who were (I suppose) either male or female, but I could not tell which. Even after exchanging a few remarks with one of them following the service I was not sure. There was also one person who I thought might be a transsexual. Or perhaps a man dressed as a woman. It was difficult to tell. The individual's voice gave no clue. It was either a low alto or a high tenor.

There were, of course, many gay and lesbian couples, and sometimes during the service they would stand with their arms around each other, or they would sit very close, just as heterosexual couples sometimes do.

Many thoughts went through my mind. One of them was that Jesus was sitting somewhere in that building, unseen but rejoicing that these children of his had gathered to worship him. Another idea that occurred to me was how much Jesus must love these people just *because* they were wounded in ways that we have not understood or been aware of. I thanked God for this place where these people could come and worship and feel accepted, even those who did not seem definitely of one sex or the other.

I felt, too, a great shame that they were worshiping separately. Because there has been no real place for them in the organized church, God had reached out and provided a church.

Suppose the Christian church could accept all these sexually anomalous people within its walls, not condemning their

139

sexuality but providing them the same care and concern provided the more orthodox heterosexual Christians. Suppose there were pastors or counselors to whom the gays or lesbians could go with their problems. For example, a lesbian has asked where a gay Christian can go for help in facing the future when a relationship has ended.[3] Most churches at present are not equipped to handle this kind of counseling.

Or suppose there were support groups within the church for gays and lesbians. How much more helpful it would be to turn to other Christians than to seek whatever solace or answers may be offered by the companionship of the gay or lesbian bar.

There are beginning to be such groups within the Catholic, Episcopal, Lutheran, and other church bodies. Often it is something of an uphill fight to find a church that will allow them to hold their meetings on the premises. A few individual gays and lesbians have made a place for themselves within the predominantly heterosexual married population of most Christian congregations, but these persons are the exception rather than the rule. Most of them have not done it as openly acknowledged gay men and women.

But suppose that a congregation included the full spectrum of sexual anomalies. What might happen? One would hope that it might be a means of encouraging a loving Christian maturity within the congregation. After all, the world is not made up exclusively of healthy, heterosexual people. There are the less-favored ones as well—the physically or emotionally crippled and the mentally retarded, as well as those who do not fall within the category of ordinary heterosexual people. They are all part of God's world, and the sooner the ordinary Christian learns to face this reality and deal with it, the better.

In time it is even possible that there would not have to be separate support groups for gays and straights. The love of Christ might conceivably so permeate the church that each side could listen with respect to the pains of those who were different from them and offer prayers for a brother or sister in trouble.

But what if children should ask their parents why the two

men (or two women) in front of them in church that morning were holding hands? It seems to me that parents would have a natural opportunity to explain to their children one of the facts of life which they are going to learn anyhow, that some people are born unable to be sexually interested in the opposite sex, only in their own sex. Most people, it could be explained to the children, are born able to be sexually interested in the opposite sex, but some people aren't.[4]

No bones about it. No big deal. If the parents aren't uptight about it, the children won't be either. And the old bogey that young people may become confused in their gender identity as they grow up has been taken care of. The statement has been included that most people *do* feel sexual interest in the opposite sex.

That day as I worshiped in that different congregation, a phrase occurred to me: reverence for life. That morning there suddenly welled up in me a reverence for the life each person there had been given, a respect for each person as a human being, no matter how odd that person might seem to me. Whatever the physical or psychological ambiguities, there was nothing that said I was a better person because I happened to be straight or because I had been born with my genital equipment matching the gender identity in my head. I was perhaps more fortunate, but might that not place a greater obligation upon me to reach out to my less-fortunate neighbor?

Besides, I had to acknowledge that I had done nothing to earn this good fortune. My sexual orientation had been given to me. By the luck of the draw (as Robert Farrar Capon has said in a different context),[5] I am straight, not gay. It is therefore not something in which I can legitimately take pride.

*　*　*　*

In the first few days after learning of Eric's homosexuality I received comfort and strength, and a promise, from the words of Isaiah 61:

> to comfort all who mourn;
> to grant to those who mourn in Zion—
> to give them a garland instead of ashes,

the oil of gladness instead of mourning,
    the mantle of praise instead of a faint spirit;. . .
They shall build up the ancient ruins,
    they shall raise up the former devastations;
they shall repair the ruined cities,
    the devastations of many generations.[6]

As I take stock of my situation today, I see that I have indeed been given a garland instead of ashes, the oil of gladness instead of mourning.

And I see something else. All my life, from the time I was allowed to go to Sunday school with my older sister, Meg (even though I was below the age when they usually accepted children), I have been deeply involved in one way or another with the church. I care intensely about the church, even though I have not always been head over heels in love with its ladies' aids, its chicken suppers, or its white-elephant and bake sales.

I see that I want, in whatever ways may be open to me, to help Christians understand the truth about homosexual persons and homosexuality so that they will no longer be fearful or condemning but can understand that what goes on in the spirit and mind and body of a gay person is not so very different from what goes on in the spirit and mind and body of a straight. The needs and desires of each side are not so very different. The love object of the relationship may be different, but the need for relationships that will build up and fulfill, not tear down and deplete, is the same.

If we could have a reverence for the life force of each individual person, if we could see him or her as of infinite value to God, what a difference it would make in our churches! What a difference it would make in our world!

Is this a valid dream?

No dream ever becomes valid until people try to put feet on the dream and make it walk.

At a time in my life, therefore, when I might begin to sneak thoughts of slowing down, pulling back, easing off, I am just beginning. All that has gone before has been the prelude, the preparation. I am about to venture forth upon what I hope may be the most significant work of my life.

I would like to help the church—individual Christians, individual congregations, denominations—begin to understand some of the whole complex tangle we term homosexuality. I would like to help draw the sting of fear, hatred, and disgust and replace it with a reverence for the individuals who live within the veil of a flesh they have not chosen. I would especially like to talk with the parents of gays and lesbians and help them accept what in many cases cannot be changed.

In order to do this I must leave my secure hideaway in Lakota and move into Minneapolis. The for-sale sign stands on my lawn. A real estate agent is looking for a house for me that is nearer those things which my new life will involve.

I am going forth to help repair the devastations of many generations. The long dark night of my soul has passed; the days of my mourning have ended. I have stepped forth, at last, into a morning of joy.

Afterword:
The Joy Holds

The last sentence of the preceding chapter was written a year and a half ago. What has happened to the "morning of joy" which seemed to surround me at that time? Was it a real, durable joy or only a fleeting emotion that evaporated when the sun grew hot?

It took me five months to find a house I wanted in the right location at a price I could afford. When I did find the house, I was fortunate enough to have a buyer eager to have my house, and I bought and sold on the same day.

I moved at the end of March 1978. The vote to keep or repeal the gay rights section of the St. Paul human rights ordinance was scheduled for April 25. In spite of the fact that I had never before taken part in any political activity except voting, I threw myself into the last frenzied days of the campaign.

Here was Dade County moved to my own front yard. The ordinance on the St. Paul books stated that gays could not be denied membership in labor unions, fired from jobs, denied housing, education, or public accommodations simply because they were gay.

But the minister of a Christian church in St. Paul had initiated the drive for the repeal of this part of the human rights ordinance—not rights of gay persons to do strange, harmful things to society but rights simply commensurate with those which heterosexual people take for granted.

Even though I had just moved and boxes and barrels were still standing everywhere, I devoted as much time as I could to the campaign. I was part of a panel of parents of gays and lesbians who held a news conference. We spent forty-five minutes reading a prepared statement, being filmed and interviewed by representatives of the St. Paul and Minneapolis media. Only presidential news conferences are reproduced in their entirety, I discovered. One-minute clips of ours appeared on radio and TV. Newspaper articles covered a little more of the proceedings.

I gave precious time to a local radio station that interviewed me at length concerning my experiences in learning that my son was gay and in dealing with this information. Because the tape of the interview unfortunately was lost, it was never aired.

I wrote letters to the editors of the St. Paul and Minneapolis newspapers. A few were published.

At the St. Paul Citizens for Human Rights headquarters I spent evenings looking up telephone numbers, folding flyers, stuffing envelopes until exhaustion from the move and the subsequent pace of my life forced me to quit. The week before the vote I rested—and cursed the limitations of my strength which kept me home instead of hanging flyers on doorknobs in St. Paul and taking part in an outdoor rally and march for gay rights.

The first political actions of my life—and we lost.

As it now stands, because of repeal a person *can* lose his or her job in St. Paul, *can* be refused membership in a labor union, *can* be turned out of her or his lodgings, *can* be denied the opportunity to buy a specific house, *can* be refused service in a restaurant or accommodations in a hotel, and *can* be denied educational opportunities—not because of any overt unseemly action (we have laws to take care of that kind of thing for both heterosexual and homosexual persons) but simply because the person is who he or she is: gay or lesbian. It is now legal to treat certain people as second-class citizens.[1]

I recently heard of a professional man who, a month after gay rights were repealed, was kicked out of the apartment where he had lived for four years. The management gave him no reason why he had to move, only a terse "get out." The ironic part is that, after ridding the apartment building of a supposedly undesirable tenant, the management rented the apartment to a heterosexual woman who is now being tried in court on a severe and gruesome child-abuse matter.

Even before I moved, I had become active in a Families of Gays and Lesbians group. Mothers and fathers of gay persons, and sometimes brothers and sisters, meet to find out more about homosexuality and to receive support from others who have gone or are going through the same experiences of learning to cope with gayness in the family.

In this group, and in other situations as well, I have talked with many parents concerning their child's sexual orientation. I can see the parents' pain. I remember the days of my own pain when I first learned of Eric's gayness. I know what they are feeling, and yet sometimes I want to say, "What's all the agony about? Look at your child. Whom do you see? A compassionate, interested, interesting person? A creative, contributing member of society? One with character and integrity? Your child is not some unwholesome, unworthy monster. Who these people share their bed with is relatively unimportant. The reasons for which it is shared *are* important. If it is an exploitive relationship, whether heterosexual or homosexual, I would be concerned for my child's values and wholeness. If there is a great deal of promiscuity, whether heterosexual or homosexual, I would be concerned. But just the fact that your child loves a person of the same sex in a genital relationship, what is that?"

I don't say this, because I know I could not have heard and absorbed those words four years ago.

It has been surprising to me to see how appealing this family group is to gay persons. They come to find out how to tell their families, or they come to get help in dealing with families who know but are still upset and largely unaccepting. They come, too, I think, just because it feels good to be around parents who are, if not totally accepting in all cases, at least making real efforts to come to terms with their children's gayness.

Before I moved, I had also joined a gay church group and had begun attending the monthly communion services. It took courage for me to go to the first meeting. On the way to the church I almost lost my nerve.

Suppose they all stand in one corner and I stand in the other corner, and all we do is stare at each other and never make contact, I thought. Maybe they'll wonder who this middle-aged woman thinks she is that they should include her in their fellowship. I decided that if the evening turned out to be a disaster, so what? I would never have to go back again.

When I reached the church, I went in. About twenty persons, all men, most of them young, were standing around in little clusters talking. They did look at me somewhat questioningly, but almost immediately a young man in a clerical collar, who turned out to be the officiating minister, detached himself from a group and came toward me.

"May I help you?" he asked. "Are you looking for someone?" He obviously thought I had gotten to the wrong place.

"I came for the communion service," I answered. "I'm the mother of a gay son. Is it all right if I stay?"

The mother of a gay son who cared enough to hunt up nonrelated gay persons? I had said the magic words. Of course I could stay.

In the communion service there is the passing of the peace. I was unprepared for the hugs and kisses at this juncture which everyone gave everyone else. It was heartwarming to me to be hugged, and in some cases kissed, by these strangers. They made no distinction between the "in" group and the strange older woman who had suddenly shown up in their midst. I had demonstrated a caring by coming. They accepted that caring and gave back their own in abundant measure.

After the service they began making arrangements to go someplace to eat. I was preparing to leave when to my surprise several of them said to me, "You'll come with us, won't you?"

I gulped. Did these young men actually want a mother type

tagging along? Or were these polite noises they had been trained to make? The amount of urging they were giving me to join them seemed to indicate that maybe they really did want me to come.

"Yes," I told them, "count me in."

I spent a very enjoyable hour and a half eating and visiting with the group. At no time did they give me the impression that they were unhappy to have me there. I was treated as an honored guest.

Since that day I don't miss a monthly communion service if I can help it. If I can't get to a service, they are concerned. Where have I been? They have missed me.

In this group, and in other gay groups in which I have found myself, I have learned that one accepting mother is worth her weight in rubies to many gay persons.

New experiences continue to come my way.

This past year I marched in the Gay Pride Week parade, helping to carry a banner which proclaimed, "Parents of Gays and Lesbians—we love our gay children." I felt a moment of fear when we discovered that a band of ten young Nazis was picketing the small park in downtown St. Paul that was our destination. "Ignore them," our leaders said, and we did. The local police were out in force that day to protect us all—the marchers, the bystanding citizens, even the Nazis. There were no confrontations. But I had a glimpse of what it means to be identified with a despised minority.

During the past year I have been invited to a number of gay parties. No doubt I have not witnessed the wilder variety, but I can attest to the fact that not every gay party is an orgy. If you were to walk into such a party, I doubt whether you could tell if the people were straight or gay. Sometimes there is a mixture of straight and gay people. Sometimes I have been the only straight person.

The interesting thing is that at a heterosexual party, which at my age largely means married couples, I am usually a fifth wheel if I am alone, or else I need an escort in order really to be one of the group. At a gay party I seem to be accepted as a whole person, just as I am. It isn't necessary for me to be accompanied by a man. Even though I come alone, I am not conspicuous. Nobody at the party is expecting everyone to be paired off. The gay community has given me an acceptance as a single person, which the heterosexual community has somehow not been able to do.

Whom do I meet at gay parties? Weirdos, queers, queens, and faggots? I have yet to meet anyone who answers those descriptions. I have met responsible, interesting, worthwhile men and women. I have met teachers, preachers, musicians, interior decorators, and clerks (both office and store). I have met publishers, hair dressers, florists, insurance salespersons, counselors, government employees, real estate salespersons, secretaries, doctors, lawyers, politicians, students, air traffic controllers, broadcasters, hospital personnel—you get the idea. I have met people who are no different from other people. I have been impressed by the quality of these people. The conversations we have had have been interesting and enjoyable.

Gay parties are one thing. The host or hostess invites congenial people. But what about gay bars? Aren't they stomach-turning dens of iniquity?

Here I must confess that bars—any bars—are not my natural milieu. Straight bars are not my favorite scene, and I have not spent any large portion of my life sitting in them. Of course, there is a wide variation even in straight bars. Some are fine, but there are also many that I wouldn't care to enter.

The same could be said of gay or lesbian bars. Friends have taken me to several, and I can't say that I saw anything different going on there from what one sees in a straight bar. The object of the behavior may be different; for instance, two men or two women may be holding hands or standing with their arms around each other, whereas in a straight bar it would be a man and a woman. But the type of behavior is similar. The friends have not taken me to any of the raunchier gay bars, and I don't care to go to those any more than I would care to set foot in a massage parlor, topless bar, or other place that degrades heterosexual sex.

149

But what of my desire to help Christians come to terms with homosexuality? Have I been able to do anything in this area?

A little. Whenever I say to any pastor or any church member, "I have a gay son," I am saying something important. I am forcing the person to grapple, at least in some very small measure, with the fact that homosexuality does happen to people they know, that it does happen to Christians, and that one person at least does not regard it as shameful information to be hidden.

Beyond my personal statement that I have a gay son, I knock on any door that comes within my reach, knowing that if I knock on enough doors, one or two are bound to open.

I have told my story to the pastors of a number of churches and to the regional leaders of my denomination. (Two years ago I left the Community of the Resurrection and joined a denominational church.)

Four gay persons and I have comprised a team which has spoken about homosexuality to a regional committee of my denomination. I have also spoken at an interdenominational seminar for clergy and ministerial students who are seeking ways to minister to gay persons and families of gays.

Just recently I volunteered to be on the committee in my congregation that is trying to come to grips with the whole matter of Christianity and sexuality, homosexuality included. As I look at the scope of the task before us, I am overwhelmed. I suddenly realize how little the Christian church has come to grips with the sexual explosion in our society today and how desperately the church needs to deal with all the sexual issues of the day, not only homosexuality.[2]

Here is a place where I can at least get a toehold. It is a place to begin. Who knows what paths may lead out from here?

*   *   *   *

And what of Eric, Brian, Barbara, Emily, and Hans now? What directions are their lives taking? How do they feel about the directions my life is taking?

They all seem to be supportive of this new person I have

become in the last several years, of the new life that has opened to me.

Eric at twenty-three is not very different from a lot of other twenty-three-year-olds. The struggles in which he is engaged have nothing to do with his gayness. They have to do with getting to know himself better, with the adjustments that come in any serious long-term relationship, with career directions, with hopes and expectations for his future.

He and Brian are still together after four years. Although there has never been any legal or religious ceremony to unite them, Brian is as much a son-in-law to me as Hans is. Canon Clinton Jones, in *Understanding Gay Relatives and Friends*, has written of a mother whose son is in a committed gay relationship. "Through her son's commitment to another person she may not have 'gained a daughter,' but perhaps she can feel she has 'gained another son.' "[3]

When I moved, Brian was on hand to help me. Eric would have been too, but he was working and Brian was not. Later they papered several rooms for me, and Brian helped me paint my bedroom. I have also sought his advice on interior decorating matters. I do indeed feel that I have gained another son. If the relationship between Eric and him were broken, I would feel as much a sense of loss as I would if I had lost a son-in-law.

Barbara is a junior in college. She has her own apartment, and we see each other occasionally. Between meetings we keep in touch by phone. She has mellowed a great deal in her feelings about Eric's homosexuality. The fact that she has rubbed elbows with gay persons at college has undoubtedly helped in this respect. She has also mellowed in her feelings about me, a development which makes me very happy.

Emily and Hans have left Chicago for a three-year stint in South America. I miss them greatly, and yet I am happy for the sense of purpose which has sent them there, happy for the new experiences of responsibility and growth which they are having. If I am honest, I must confess that I hope they don't fall so in love with South America that they remain there indefinitely.

151

But if they do, I hope I shall respect their choice and not try by subtle means to draw them home again.

*   *   *   *

I do not want to end without saying a special word about lesbians. In the beginning it was much easier for me to deal with gay men than with lesbians. I felt a lot less threatened.

My first real contact with a lesbian was at the initial Families of Gays and Lesbians meeting I attended. When we went around the circle introducing ourselves, I could feel myself tighten involuntarily when one said, "I'm Joan, and I'm a lesbian," and another woman said, "I'm Billie, and I'm lesbian."

As the months passed I grew fond of these two women. I came to appreciate their integrity, to share their ups and downs in their careers, to miss them when they weren't at a meeting. Since then, as I have moved about in the gay community, I have come into contact with a large number of other lesbians. I have even on occasion become brave enough to hug one or another lesbian friend without being afraid that I may be sending some unwitting message. I have come to see them first and foremost as persons, as friends and acquaintances. The fact that they happen to be lesbian is not terribly important. I know now that they aren't really so very different from me.

*   *   *   *

Was the "morning of joy" only a fleeting moment in my life?

Joy does not mean an absence of frustrations or pain. Nor does it mean that I skim easily along over the surface of a calm life with the sun perpetually shining and everything falling neatly and effortlessly into place. I still stumble. I still struggle. I still agonize. But underneath flows a steady current. My life has meaning and purpose, and they are the source of my joy.

Viktor Frankl has said, "Suffering ceases to be suffering in some way at the moment it finds a meaning."[4]

I have found that meaning. The sufferings through which I have passed have not been wasted. They have been stepping-stones to fuller, more outgoing living.

With tremendous affirmation I can say, "The joy holds."

Notes

Unless otherwise indicated, scripture quotations are from *Revised Standard Version of the Bible*, copyright 1946, 1952 and © 1971 by the Division of Christian Education, National Council of Churches, and are used by permission.

Chapter 2   The Long Night

1. Psalm 23:4, KJV.
2. Isaiah 53:4.
3. Leviticus 18:22.
4. 1 Corinthians 6:9-10.
5. David and Don Wilkerson, *The Untapped Generation* (Grand Rapids, Mich.: Zondervan, 1971), p. 109.

Chapter 3   "My Son, My Son!"

1. Lewis Carroll, *Alice in Wonderland* (New York: Grosset & Dunlap, 1946), p. 60.
2. 2 Samuel 18:33, KJV.

Chapter 4   The First Step

1. Catherine Marshall, *Something More* (New York: Mc-Graw-Hill, 1974), p. 106.
2. Exodus 20:5.

Chapter 5   Battle Plans

1. Merlin R. Carothers, *Power in Praise,* ed. Jorunn Oftedal Ricketts (Plainfield, N.J.: Logos International, 1972).
2. Jeremiah 32:17, adapted from the *King James Version.*
3. Luke 1:37.
4. Exodus 20:5; italics added.

Chapter 6   Tom and Meta

1. Isaiah 61:1-3.
2. Isaiah 61:4.

Chapter 7   Summit Conference

1. Morton T. Kelsey, *God, Dreams and Revelations* (Minneapolis: Augsburg, 1974), p. 209.

Chapter 8   Eric's "Friend"

1. 2 Corinthians 6:14.

Chapter 10   Glimpses Beneath the Surface

1. Luke 18: 11.

Chapter 11   No Easy Answers

1. Irving Bieber, *The New York Times Magazine,* December 28, 1975, p. 19.
2. In the years since reading Dr. Bieber's book I have become acquainted with some fathers and homosexual sons who *do* have a very good relationship. I also realize that the study, which was begun in 1952, was initiated at a time when the perception of homosexuality was very different from today's understanding of it. A third factor, one which is most important to remember, is that the statistics came from that segment of the population which was hurting enough to seek psychoanalytic treatment. Homosexual men who were not experiencing deep

problems were therefore not included in the sampling.

3. Irving Bieber et al., *Homosexuality: A Psychoanalytic Study* (New York: Basic Books, Inc., 1962), pp. 60-61, 64, 65, 67, 198, 201.

4. See C. G. Jung, *Two Essays in Analytical Psychology,* tr. R. F. C. Hull (New York: World, 1967), pp. 198-224. Emma Jung has also explained this concept in *Animus and Anima: Two Essays,* tr. Cary F. Baines (New York: Spring Publications, 1957).

5. 1 Corinthians 6:9-10.

6. Theodore Isaac Rubin, *The Angry Book* (New York: Collier Books, 1970), p. 23.

7. Clinton R. Jones, *What About Homosexuality?* (New York: Thomas Nelson, Inc., 1972), pp. 16-17.

8. Bieber, *Homosexuality,* p. 278.

9. Jones, *What About Homosexuality?* p. 17.

10. John 10:10, *The Bible in Today's English Version* (New York: American Bible Society, 1971).

Chapter 12   Rocks

1. Agnes Sanford, *Behold Your God* (St. Paul: Macalester Park Publishing Company, 1958), p. 111.

2. Ephesians 4:26, KJV.

3. *Roget's International Thesaurus,* wrath (New York: Thomas Y. Crowell, 1946).

4. Matthew 5:21.

5. Theodore Isaac Rubin, *The Angry Book* (New York: Collier Books, 1970), p. 31.

6. Ibid., p. 163.

7. Ibid., p. 164.

8. John 8:32.

9. 1 John 3:15.

10. 1 Corinthians 11:24, KJV.

11. John 10:10, *The Bible in Today's English Version* (New York: American Bible Society, 1971). I have substituted "you" for "they."

12. 1 Corinthians 13:12.

Chapter 13 "My Wounded Ones"

1."Just as I Am," by Charlotte Elliott.
2. John 8:7.
3. John 3:16.
4. Matthew 9:12-13.
5. Matthew 21:31.

Chapter 14 From Judgment to Love

1. Matthew 9:9.
2. Luke 5:28.

Chapter 15 Butchina

1. C. G. Jung, *Analytical Psychology: Its Theory and Practice* ("The Tavistock Lectures"; New York: Random House, 1970), p. 192.
2. Helen M. Luke, *The Way of Woman, Ancient and Modern* (Three Rivers, Mich.: Apple Farm Community), p. 4.

Chapter 16 Troy Perry

1. Troy Perry, *The Lord Is My Shepherd and He Knows I'm Gay*, as told to Charles L. Lucas (Los Angeles: Nash Publishing Corporation, 1972), p. 217. Copyright 1972. Reprinted by permission of Nash Publishing Corporation.
2. Ibid., p. 146.
3. Ibid., p. 220.
4. Ibid., p. 172.
5. Ibid., pp. 68, 70.
6. Ibid., p. 5.
7. Ibid., p. 214.
8. Ibid., p. 120.
9. Ibid., pp. 193-95.
10. Ibid., pp. 156, 168, 172.
11. Ibid., pp. 210-11.

Chapter 17 Sinner or Victim?

1. James Harrison, "The Dynamics of Sexual Anxiety," *Christianity and Crisis*, vol. 37, nos. 9 and 10, May 30 and June 13, 1977.

2. Donald Goergen, in *The Sexual Celibate* (New York: Seabury Press, 1974), has written a thought-provoking analysis of the terms "homosexuality" and "heterosexuality" as compared to homoerotic, homogenital, and monosexual sexuality.

3. Ruth Tiffany Barnhouse, *Homosexuality: A Symbolic Confusion* (New York: Seabury Press, 1977), p. 22.

4. Charles W. Socarides, "Homosexuality Is Not Just an Alternative Life Style," *Male and Female: Christian Approaches to Homosexuality*, ed. Ruth Tiffany Barnhouse and Urban T. Holmes, III (New York: Seabury Press, 1976), p. 144.

5. Morton T. Kelsey, "The Homosexual and the Church," *Sex: Thoughts for Contemporary Christians*, ed. Michael J. Taylor, S.J. (Garden City, N.Y.: Doubleday, 1972), p. 224.

6. Lawrence J. Hatterer, *Changing Homosexuality in the Male* (New York: McGraw-Hill, 1970), p. 26.

7. Bob Sutton, "Homosexuality," *New Wine* magazine, vol. 6, no. 6, June 1974, p. 25.

8. John Money and Anke A. Ehrhardt, *Man and Woman, Boy and Girl* (Baltimore: Johns Hopkins Press, 1974), p. 1.

9. Ibid., p. 2.

10. Ibid.

11. Leviticus 20:13.

12. From the Covenant adopted at the International Congress on World Evangelization held at Lausanne, Switzerland, July 16-25, 1974.

Chapter 18 New Paths Through the Desert

In addition to the specific references given below, several articles contributed greatly to my thinking. They are "A Biblical Perspective on Homosexuality," by David Bartlett, published in *Foundations*, vol. 20, no. 2, April-June 1977;

"Homosexuality and the Church," by James B. Nelson, published in *Christianity and Crisis*, April 4, 1977; additional notes on "Homosexuality and the Church," by James B. Nelson, *Christianity and Crisis*, May 30 and June 13, 1977. The Sodom and Gomorrah story is found in Genesis 19:1-11.

1. The Ordination of a Priest, *The Book of Common Prayer* (Proposed) of the Episcopal Church, p. 526.

2. The Rite of Confirmation, *Hymnal and Liturgies of the Moravian Church (Unitas Fratrum)*, 1923, p. 32.

3. M. Esther Harding, *Woman's Mysteries* (New York: Harper & Row, 1976), p. 57.

4. Leviticus 12:2-5.

5. Leviticus 18:22.

6. Romans 1:23-27.

7. Jeremiah 31:33.

8. W. Norman Pittenger, *Making Sexuality Human* (New York: The Pilgrim Press, 1970), especially the chapter "The Homosexual Expression of Sexuality."

Chapter 19   Integrating the Wolf

1. Peggy Way, "Homosexual Counseling as a Learning Ministry," *Christianity and Crisis*, vol. 37, nos. 9 and 10, May 30 and June 13, 1977. In this chapter I have adapted some of Dr. Way's article to round out our conversation. It was, in fact, not necessary for her to say a few of these things during the interview because I had already read them in her article.

2. Lawrence J. Hatterer, *Changing Homosexuality in the Male* (New York: McGraw-Hill, 1970), p. 1.

3. Alan W. Jones, "When Is a Homosexual Not a Homosexual?" *Anglican Theological Review*, vol. 59, no. 2, April 1977, p. 184.

4. Arno Karlen, *Sexuality and Homosexuality* (New York: W. W. Norton & Co., 1971), p. 99.

5. Ibid., pp. 88-89.

6. Ibid., p. 609.

7. *Newsweek*, June 20, 1977, p. 27.

8. *Newsweek,* June 6, 1977, pp. 22, 16.

9. *Minneapolis Star,* June 10, 1977.

10. *Time,* June 20, 1977, p. 60.

11. Everyone is familiar with the double yellow triangles, signifying the Star of David, which Jews were required to wear in Nazi Germany. The general public is not as familiar with the single pink triangle which the Nazis forced homosexual persons to wear. Pages 313-15 in Karlen's book *Sexuality and Homosexuality* give an interesting background to this public degradation of homosexual persons. It is well known that millions of Jews perished in concentration camp ovens. It is not as well known that huge numbers of homosexual persons also perished this way.

12. Robert A. Johnson, *He!* (King of Prussia, Pa.: Religious Publishing Co., 1974), p. 72.

13. *Minneapolis Star Saturday Magazine,* December 3, 1977, p. 6.

14. Genesis 1:27-28, 31; Ephesians 5:21-32.

Chapter 20 Morning of Joy

1. Morton Kelsey, *Myth, History and Faith* (New York: Paulist/Newman Press, 1974), p. 165.

2. Dr. Charles Silverstein, *A Family Matter* (New York: McGraw-Hill, 1977), p. 96.

3. Nancy E. Krody, "Woman, Lesbian, Feminist, Christian," *Christianity and Crisis,* vol. 37, nos. 9 and 10, May 30 and June 13, 1977, p. 133.

4. Originally I used the word love instead of the phrase "be sexually interested in" in this passage. A gay friend, however, pointed out that he does love women, though not in a sexual way. The problem arises because we generally use the one word love to cover so many different aspects of emotion.

5. Robert Farrar Capon, *The Supper of the Lamb* (Garden City, N.Y.: Doubleday, 1967), p. 146. Father Capon was writing about the well-fed people of the world versus the hungry ones, but it seems to me that we receive many things simply because of the

family and environment into which we are born, which we had no hand in choosing.

6. Isaiah 61:2-4.

Afterword: The Joy Holds

1. If I have learned one thing this year, it is that gays need not lead tragic, unfulfilled lives. As a matter of fact, most of them don't. Most of them are as happy or as unhappy as their straight counterparts. The difference between them and straight persons lies not in the happiness or unhappiness of their lives. It lies in the political and social strictures against which gay persons must continue to labor.

2. Dr. James B. Nelson's book, *Embodiment: An Approach to Sexuality and Christian Theology* (Minneapolis: Augsburg, 1978), deals with this whole matter in detail. For those who are especially concerned about a conflict between the church or religion and homosexuality, I highly recommend his chapter 8, "Gayness and Homosexuality: Issues for the Church." The book is also available from The Pilgrim Press.

3. Clinton R. Jones, *Understanding Gay Relatives and Friends* (New York: Seabury Press, 1978), p. 16.

4. Viktor Frankl, *Man's Search for Meaning* (Boston: Beacon Press, 1965), p. 115.